OPERATING SYSTEM ANALYSIS AND DESIGN

OPERATING SYSTEM ANALYSIS AND DESIGN

by

Leo J. Cohen

SPARTAN BOOKS

NEW YORK • WASHINGTON

Library of Congress Catalog Card No.: 79-118984

International Standard Book Number: 0-87671-164-6

Printed in the United States of America.

Sole Distributors in Great Britain, the British Commonwealth, and the Continent of Europe:

Macmillan and Company, Ltd.
4 Little Essex Street
London, W. C. 2

CONTENTS

CHAPTER 1

INTRODUCTION

THE SUBJECT OF this work is the operating system and quite properly it should begin with a definition of that term. A formal, generally applicable definition, however, is difficult in the best of circumstances and impossible to achieve within the boundary of a handful of words.

Perhaps the major source of this difficulty in defining the term "operating system" derives from the nature of the digital computer itself. That is, the purpose of the digital computer, its CPU, its core memory, and all of its peripheral equipments, is the execution of programs. Some of these programs are written by the day-to-day users of the system and are loosely referred to as the "application programs." Others of these programs have been written by somebody else, at an earlier time, and are in some vague sense a part of the system, much as the magnetic tapes and CPU are part of the system. The general term "system software" has been used to describe these computer programs, and more recently the possibly more suggestive term "firmware" has come into vogue. The operating system is a computer program as well, and in recent experience may very well be the largest program that is applied to the computer, appearing as an aggregate of programs that are considered to be part of the "software" or "firmware."

Such terms are useful in conversation and perhaps in high-level sales, but do little to clearly delineate the operative roll of the entity called the operating system as opposed to both the remaining "software" and the application programs. It is therefore a purpose of the present work to develop technological formalisms that will provide a means for clearly distinguishing the operating system from all other programs applied to a given computer. This will take some doing, and the reader's indulgence is begged while the term "operating system" is temporarily employed. Chapters 2, 3, and 5 contribute to this objective, while in Chapter 6 we shall describe a certain basic set of functional units that must belong to any operating system if programmers are to use the computer at all. For the remainder of this introductory discussion, however, we consider only general characteristics and what might be thought of as anthropological origin.

Assemblers

Perhaps the earliest programming system made available to the general user was UNIVAC generalized programming (GP) for the UNIVAC I, and later, UNIVAC II computers. The major characteristic of this early assembly language was its representation of data and locations in terms of symbolic references. There can be little argument as to the degree of usefulness of this assembler from the user's point of view relative to writing absolute addresses. In addition, this assembler gave the user access to all of the facilities available via instructions in the computer hardware, and therefore did not curtail his use of any part of the system that would have been available had he programmed in machine language. Conversationally speaking, at this stage of development the assembler program was the "software" for the computer system. It is, of course, difficult to accredit such software as an "operating system," but almost immediate additions made to assembler capabilities were at least a positive step in that direction.

An early enhancement of UNIVAC GP allowed the user a limited facility for modifying operands and calculating addresses symbolically during the assembly operation as well as at execution time. This added a surprisingly broad dimension to the flexibility of programming in GP and became a standard characteristic for virtually all assemblers that have been developed in the industry. Another enhancement was the introduction of a set of pseudoinstructions that transcended the available instruction repertoire and gave the programmer a powerful tool for accomplishing potentially sophisticated programming. These pseudoinstructions were, of course, translated by the assembler program during the assembly operation, with each such instruction generally resulting in a set of corresponding machine language instructions. Thus again, the design of the assembler program has been expanded to offer the user a larger degree of capability, but thus far without any curtailment of access to the available facilities of the system.

Batch Control

At this stage of its development, the assembler provided the user with an ever-widening spectrum of facilities for the preparation of sophisticated solutions to computer problems. The result of an assembly is a collection of executable instructions output on some medium such as tape or cards. These instructions are the assembler translation of the mnemonic, pseudo- and macroinstructions prepared by the user, plus subprograms drawn from a tape or card library during the assembly process and linked to the user's program according to his specifications in the pseudoinstructions designated for that purpose. In addition, the assembler has output a short section of code designed to facilitate the loading of the assembled program into the computer system for execution.

We thus arrive at a point where a growing number of users seek the use of the computer system for both assembly operations and execution of assembled programs. Therefore, the development of the concept of a "job" and the design and implementation of techniques for controlling the execution of a sequence of jobs in a batch consisting of an arbitrary mixture of assemblies and executions was natural. To accomplish this operation required a special program, and it was necessary to conceive of the hardware computer system as being strongly associated with this program. This was certainly a major step beyond the assembler and marks the advent of "system software."

There is a particular characteristic of this early type of software which should be noted. During the execution of a particular job in the batch, i.e., assembly, or execution of an assembled program, either no traces or only the smallest remnant of this system software was present in the computer memory. That is, virtually the entire memory was made available for the execution of the current job. In fact, one objective was to reserve only a minimum amount of the system's facilities for this software, thus necessitating its absence from the memory during job execution and often retiring it to a single magnetic tape drive. The mode of operation of this type of software was therefore as follows. At the end of execution of the current job, sufficient programming would be supplied to initiate the loading of the software and cause a transfer of control to these programs. The execution of this software would then cause the prefatory information for the next job to be examined, determining whether it was an assembly or program execution. In the former case the software would initiate the loading of the assembler programs usually carried on the same tape as the software itself. Once loaded, the assembler would then carry out its operations relative to the assembly language programming, determined to be the nature of the next job of the batch. When the assembly operation terminated, loading of the software programs would again be initiated and the process repeated until all jobs in the batch had been passed through the system.

If the software programs determine that the next job in the batch is a program execution, then loading of that program is initiated, and control of the system given over to these routines. At the termination of program execution, loading of the software programs is again initiated and the process continues as described above.

Thus the sequential execution of a batch of jobs is accomplished by interleaving an execution of the control program. This type of software is referred to as a batch control system.

Though the batch control programs are not present in the computer memory during the execution of a job, it is clear that they have left traces, however minimal, in these job programs. Considering first the assembler program, it is evident that its implementation must have included sufficient instructions for initiating the loading of the batch processing routines after the assembly operations are complete. It is also evident that this function must appear as a set of instructions added at the proper place in each of the assembled programs to be executed. Thus, we see that the appearance of the batch processing system has had at least two influences on the implementation of any assembler that runs under its control. However, a third, and for our purposes much more important, influence is immediately apparent.

The batch processing system requires that information suitable for distinguishing between the two types of jobs precede each job in the batch. This information designates the nature of the job to be received and indicates to the batch control system what actions it must take in order to properly initiate the required function. The form of specification for this information is generally considered as the "job request language," and in virtually all of today's computer systems we find that this is a language usually quite different from that language made available for the preparation of programs. The important point of distinction between these two types of languages is that the purpose of the programming language is to direct and exercise the language processor at assembly time, and the computer system at execution time. On the other hand, the job request language is aimed more particularly at directing the activities of the system software.

Compilers

A compiler language is a programming technique whose differences with respect to the assembly language is usually represented as the difference between a "problem oriented" and "machine oriented" language. A machine oriented language, as has been mentioned earlier, is designed to give the user full access to all of the computer system's facilities. Thus, the programming unit at its lowest level is the mnemonic instruction. On the other hand, the problem oriented language is designed to provide the user with a set of logical functions that can be associated more or less directly with the flow chart conventions adopted in the preparation of the computer solution of a problem. In an informal way, therefore, the compiler language statement may be thought of as the basic programming element.

Perhaps the most obvious effect of the compiler with respect to an operating system is the implementation of I/O operations. In general the user has available a set of statements for reading and writing relative to data files that are carried on media external to the core memory of the system. In a compiler language, the user's reference to the data to be transferred is usually symbolic and in terms of structures and formats that have been previously declared by other compiler statements. The actual programming necessary to collect or disseminate data relative to the core memory in order to execute an I/O function, and to carry out the required data transfer relative to the peripheral device involved, is often of such a nature that it is best accomplished as a subprogram. Furthermore, this subprogramming can be made standard for all users of a given compiler, so that rather than generating a subprogram for I/O operations with each compilation, the required programming can be loaded as a standard package at the time when the compiled program is brought into the computer's memory for execution.

In this case it is clear that a major responsibility of the compiler is to insert interface coding into the compiled program, at the point of occurrence of the I/O statements. This interface coding links the user's program to the standard subroutines for I/O handling at execution time. These standard subroutines are today incorporated into operating systems as the "I/O package," and led naturally to the inclusion of an "interrupt handler" as well.

The I/O package was the seed pellet injected into the gathering cloud of ingenuity hovering over the computer industry. This was in 1958 or thereabouts, and resulted in a veritable rainstorm of software features that were soon followed by gusty winds often referred to as the "third generation." The storm continued unabated, and what was originally a welcome shower of valuable ideas became a torrent threatening to wash the programmer away in a rising tide of manuals and technical jargon. And now, in these somewhat abating years, certain things, such as octal patches and a first name relationship with the operator on the computer floor, are gone forever.

In the clearing atmosphere the presence of an enormous inventory of excellent ideas and techniques is quite evident, if only the observer will look through the jungle of "features" to sort them out, at least insofar as the operating system is concerned. Therein lie the basic objectives of this book: to determine the fundamental properties of operating systems and to develop tools that are applicable to their formal design and analyses.

Of particular concern is "multiprogramming" operating systems. Deferring a formal definition until later chapters, let us say for the moment that multiprogramming means the execution of a multiplicity of programs "all at once" rather than "one at a time" by the computer. The software entity required to accomplish this is the operating system, and throughout this book our attention will be centered on those programs of the computer system that contribute to this objective. Explicitly excluded will be other so-called sytems software such as the sort-merge generator, the compiler, the assembler, and programmer-panaceas similar to the almost ancient and soon to be forgotten (*sic*) 1401 multiutility package.

This is not to say that such programs do not have their place, and indeed an important one, in the overall computing environment, but rather establishes at the outset our point of view here that that place is not with the operating system. We thus strip away layers of program that are only confusing fat over the muscle of the prime topic, and restrict our investigations to fundamental concepts and tools necessary to the design and analysis of operating systems capable of multiprogramming.

CHAPTER 2

DESIGN OBJECTIVES

Introduction

A COMPUTING SYSTEM is a mixture of individually complex logical, mechanical, and electrical elements. Its performance is an interactive function of all elements jointly, and, therefore, the meaning of the term "system performance" is entirely dependent on the interests of the person employing it. Thus, for example, to the peripheral equipment engineer, mean-time-between-failure is an essential ingredient of system performance. For the user of the computer system, particularly for the programmer employing a high-level language, system performance has meaning only in terms of ease of access to it various facilities such as files and devices, the accuracy and utility of system error diagnostic messages, and job "turn around time." On the other hand, the system's management sees performance in terms of degree of utilization of the various equipments, and simultaneously must be concerned with performance from the user's point of view.

It is immediately clear that for a given computer configuration the interest of the hardware engineer in system performance is truly academic with respect to the performance sought by the users and management. That is to say, the system's users must accept and, in many cases put up with the performance of the hardware unless it becomes so abysmal that necessary checking and testing by the software begins to make serious inroads into performance from everyone's point of view. However, our concern in this work is with the operating system and the links it forms between the users, represented by their programs, and the logical capabilities of the hardware of the system. We must necessarily assume in this that the performance of the hardware is satisfactory, and we therefore center our concern on questions of system performance from the points of view of both the system's management and the system's users.

Performance Criteria

Over a given period of operation, say one hour, there are precisely 3,600 seconds of CPU time available. During this period of operation, these 3,600 CPU seconds will be distributed to the application programs that execute in this period, and to the operating system programs that assist these executions. Any of the 3,600 CPU seconds that are not distributed in this fashion are then marked down to "idle time." This is the total time in the period of observation during which the system had nothing to do and was awaiting the arrival of its next job.

The number of CPU seconds distributed to application programs in a given time period will be referred to as the "application program CPU load." It should be noted that if a given set of application programs are to be passed through the computing system, i.e. from start of job to termination, then each will require that the CPU facility of the system be assigned to it for a certain amount of time. That is, if a given set of application programs is to pass through the system in a given time period, then it determines an amount of application program CPU load, in terms of CPU seconds, that must be supplied by the computing system.

In foregoing discussions we have implied the division of all programs using the computer system into two categories. The first of these is the application programs, and all other programs we will lump under the heading of "operating system programs." This is hardly an adequate definition of the operating system, but for the purpose of discussing performance criteria it is more than sufficient. This is due to the fact that the number of CPU seconds available in a time period of observation is fixed, and the three distribution categories mentioned earlier—application, operating system, idle—are exhaustive and mutually exclusive. Therefore, when an application program is not being executed and the system is not idling, i.e. there are jobs to be done, then the programs under execution must be associated with the operating system. Execution of operating system programs requires the assignment of the CPU facility, so that the operating system may then be said to exert a CPU load on the system as well. Clearly however, the CPU load exerted by the operating system is in response to the CPU load created as a requirement on the system by the application programs.

On the assumption that the computing system has to be paid for by its users, it is reasonable to assume that the application program portion of the system's use would be paid for by them in amounts proportionate to their individual contribution to the aggregate application program CPU load. They must, in addition, jointly support the cost of executing the operating system. That is, the execution of the application programs is associated with a general overhead cost that appears in the form of operating system CPU load. This justifies referring to the operating system CPU load as "overhead" or "system overhead." Of course, the existence of idle time implies an available CPU load, the sale of which to other users would lessen the joint system overhead burden on the current users. Clearly, however, the cost to the individual user prorated on his program's contribution to application load would remain the same. That is, the individual application load exerted by programs executing in the system does not change because of the number of such programs using it. But the time that the user waits for his job to complete may indeed change as a function of the number of application programs seeking the system's facilities. This is distinct from the number of CPU seconds the application program may require in order to complete, and it reflects the fact that in a busy multiple access environment where the system facilities are being sought simultaneously by a number of application programs, delays in the continued execution of a specific program will very likely occur.

The result might be that the "job turn around time" may vary quite dramatically as a function of the number of concurrent users of the system's facilities. Thus, a computing system may provide its current users with a satisfactory turn around time but at a burdensome overhead cost. Suppose that in such a situation a substantial amount of idle time is available, so that new users of the system would be welcomed. A possible consequence then is that the increase in overhead due to the increased activity of the system is more than offset by the number of users sharing the cost of that overhead. However, the additional delays created by the heavier traffic due to the increased number of application programs seeking the system's facilities may so elongate the individual turn around time for the former users of the system as to make the savings in overhead dollars unacceptable.

Another useful criteria for system performance is "memory load." Let us suppose that the core memory allocation unit is the word, and that the memory available for distribution to application programs is, say, 40 K words. Then over the time period of one hour, the memory would make 40 $K \times$ 3,600 word-seconds available to application programs. If a particular application program required 3,000 words of core memory and its turn around time was two minutes, then it would have exerted an application program memory load of 3,000 $\times$ 120 word-seconds on the system.

Memory load performance is a useful criteria for linking the "interior performance" (execution efficiency) to the "exterior performance" (turn around time). Each application program remains in the memory, occupying its assigned locations and aggregating memory load, until it completes. Thus, individual memory load is the product of memory space by turn around time. On the other hand, there is a limit to the amount of available memory load in a given period so that efficient performance by the operating system is tantamount to conservation of memory load, and, thereby, improvement of turn around time.

Interior Goals

The owner or management of the computing system is charged with financial responsibility for that system. It is management that must make the monthly payments. However, when there are only a few users exerting individually light CPU loads there is an aggregate amount of idle time. Since it is not likely that the users will put up with being charged the cost for the entire system it becomes necessary for management to support a certain part of the cost, which is to say that idle time is expense for management, and therefore management will seek to sell available idle time.

Another point of view is that the salable commodity available from a computing system is its idle time. An increase in the total application program CPU load corresponds to a decrease in idle time and to an increase in overhead time as well. This implies then that the basic "interior" or management goal for the design of operating systems is the distribution of the facilities of the computer, its CPU, memory and peripheral devices, to the various application programs seeking them, but in such a fashion as to minimize the overhead cost in so doing. The objective is to be able to handle the largest possible number of application programs concurrently with the least possible increase in the cost of operation, or system overhead.

A second way of saying this is that a fundamental interior goal of the operating system is to maximize application program utilization of the CPU facility. This end is served in part by maximizing the number of programs concurrently resident in the system. This lowers the probability of situations where all resident programs are seeking facilities other than the CPU, such as channels, devices, files, etc., leaving the CPU to cycle unused for relatively long periods of time. Equally important, however, is an internal structuring of the operating system, particularly that portion that will be referred to as the "executive," so that the information with which it must deal in organizing the execution activities of the several application programs resident in the system is concisely and directly available so as to minimize the operating system CPU load. Minimizing the operating system CPU load makes more idle time available, and consequently raises the number of CPU seconds that can be made available to users. The total number of CPU seconds supplied to application CPU load in the period of concern will be referred to as the "throughput" for that period.

There is another interior goal for operating system design that is directly related to management's concern with throughput. This is the throughput performance of the entire system of peripheral equipments. The execution of an application program may be thought of as a file transfer operation, moving the data in certain input files to certain output files and involving a time delay for the processing of that data during its transfer. In this sense then, the application program is not finished until all file transfer operations that it initiates have been completed, so that any delay in the file transfer activity due to congestion at, say, a data channel among several competing application programs, will be a delay in the turn around time of that program. Consequently, that program will spend more time in the memory, using the occupied memory locations for that additional period of time and increasing the memory load it exerts on the system.

This is clearly at odds with the management goal of increasing the number of users of the system since the greater the number of users, the higher the probability of interference at commonly sought I/O facilities, and consequently the lengthening of individual turn around time. There is clearly little that design can do about this, short of operating all of the peripheral facilites at their maximum rates and distributing the devices and access to them in such a fashion as to avoid stop-start time penalties (magnetic tape, printers, card readers) or excessive arm movements (disk and card random access devices). Furthermore, the operating system must be concerned that peripheral devices assigned to application programs are left idle because those application programs are not given sufficient access to the CPU facility to allow them to exercise these assigned I/O devices.

The foregoing suggests that an important interior goal for operating system design from the point of view of management is the maximization of per device throughput, and maximization of the simultaneity of device use. This topic is the central concern of the next chapter. Chapters 4 and 9 are devoted to design methods that allow the interior goals discussed in this section to be realized.

Executive—First Definition

If the computer system is to achieve certain objectives deemed to be desirable by its management, then the effort will have to be made by a computer program. Noting that a large number of the described performance criteria are germane to the so-called interior design goals, it becomes clear that the computer program designated for achieving these goals has a reasonably well defined task to accomplish. That is, a computer program is required to manage the selection of an application program to which to assign the CPU facility of the system. In addition, it must also manage the order of assignment of all peripheral equipments in the input-output chain to application programs seeking simultaneous access to them. We shall refer to this computer program of the operating system as the "executive."

It is particularly important to recognize that the executive is but one of a number of programs that make up an operating system. More specifically, in this work the term "executive" is applied to those programs of the operating system that are designed to implement the two above described functions, i.e. distribution of the CPU facility and the I/O facilities to the several application programs resident in the system.

We shall later define a logical entity to be known as the "transaction." The transaction represents an application program. In actuality it is a label used by the operating system in general, and the executive program in particular, to identify the user and his programs during their execution. It may be said then, that the executive is that program of the operating system that manipulates transactions, i.e. executions so that the interior goals of minimized overhead, maximized CPU utilization, maximum throughput per device, and maximum device simultaneity are approximated.

Exterior Goals

As mentioned earlier, the user tends to measure the performance of the system in much more qualitative and subjective terms than management. In particular, he is concerned with the language set necessary to the acceptance of his jobs by the system, and the way in which his hard copy or "presentation outputs" appear, and with what rapidity. Moreover, the system's users are very much concerned with the average time it takes to turn their jobs around. Clearly, the performance of the system from the user's point of view is a necessary, even though difficult to measure, concern of computer system management, for a dissatisfied customer is certainly no customer at all after his business has been taken elsewhere. The performance of the system, as seen by the users from the outside looking in, therefore suggests certain "exterior goals" to be achieved by the system's design.

It is evident that if users are to be able to initiate jobs in the computing system, and are to receive hard copy, or presentation results from the computing system then certain other computer programs are required. These programs will respond to whatever method the system makes available for acknowledging the presence of the user's job on an external input device, such as the card reader. They will then bring in the job description or job control language, interpret this description into a set of programs to be loaded in order to accomplish the job required, and will then carry out the necessary program loadings. This sequence of events will generally be described as the "acceptance function" of the operating system. Put another way, the operating system as a collection of computer programs will include a subset of programs designed to implement the logical activities required to accomplish this acceptance function.

Obviously the more immediate the response to the first notification of a job's presence, the better. That is, the user would prefer to see his job request read in early even though the job acceptance is delayed in internal queues. The alternative is to allow the job request to wait outside, in full view, until the system is ready for it.

Once it is received, the next step in the acceptance is translation of the job request language into machinable terms that are usable by the remainder of the system. If the job request language is particularly broad or difficult, then so also will be its translation. In such circumstances, the execution time of the translation programs may be of serious concern, particularly if these programs can only be used sequentially, and with all other multiprogramming activities intervened. Thus an especially important design goal for the acceptance functions of the operating system might be in organizing the job request translation programs as reentrant codes capable of being multiprogrammed.

During the execution of the user's application programs, output will be produced for low speed sequential devices such as printers, card punches, and so on. In a multiprogramming environment it is generally the case that such "presentation data" produced by an application program is not routed directly to the required device, since it is very likely in use by some other program under concurrent execution. The general approach is to pass such output to a large random access memory, using it as an intermediate buffer for the low speed presentation device. A second function will later bring the presentation data from this external buffer back into the computer system, from which point it can then be placed on the presentation device. The programs of the operating system designed to implement these "presentation functions" will be referred to as the "presentation portion" of the operating system.

Because of the great disparity usually found between the ability of presentation devices to produce output and the ability of the main frame to create output for production, it is quite likely that the busy system will never really catch up. On the other hand, nothing is more frustrating to the programmer who has been told that his job is completed and awaiting its turn at the printer than to see that printer sitting idle or running at a painfully inefficient rate. It is therefore necessary not only to design the output function of the presentation portion so that it is fast (the time to produce a single unit, e.g. one line of output is the absolute maximum), but also to incorporate it into the system so that it may gain control rapidly enough to operate the device at maximum efficiency.

Operating System—First Definition

Our approach will be to conceive of the operating system as a set of computer programs designed to implement the three general functions associated with the acceptance, executive, and presentation portions described in the foregoing. In later chapters, we shall adopt the point of view that the application programs, as well as the operating system programs, may be thought of as facilities of the system, and that the representative of the user in the computing system is not his programs but rather his "transaction," i.e. a logical entity that dynamically stands for the user during his passage through the system, including the execution of his application programs. It is this logical entity, the transaction, that is manipulated by the operating system. That is, transactions representing the user are passed into the acceptance portion of the operating system and through it to the executive, at which point the transaction is associated with application programs that have been loaded in the course of its acceptance. The executive then manipulates all concurrent transactions in the system to determine the dynamic distribution of the CPU and I/O facilities. As a user transaction continues its execution of (passage through) application programs, it may generate output destined for presentation devices. This output is collected by the presentation portion of the operating system on a random access device until the required presentation device becomes available. At this point the presentation output may be undertaken, and on its completion we may say that the user transaction has completed its passage through the presentation portion of the operating system, and thereby, through the entire system. We may therefore think of a job as the passage of a user transaction through all portions of the operating system.

It should be noted that in the foregoing description of the operating system, the so-called "executive" is one of the several programs of the operating system, and is furthermore defined as implementing specific operating system functions as described earlier. Thus, the executive belongs to the operating system, and in the present work is not to be confused with it.

Logical Segregation by Hardware

In the preceding paragraphs we have discussed certain functions of the operating system as belonging to it. We have then gone on to define the operating system as that set of programs which implement the acceptance, executive, and presentation portions of the operating system's logic. This suggests that all programs in the computer system fall into one of two categories; a program either belongs to the set of programs implementing the operating system, or does not. We shall refer to this latter category of programs as applications.

Consider now the execution of an application program. The job associated with the execution of the program has been passed through the acceptance portion of the operating system, resulting in this program having core memory space allocated and being loaded into the memory. The executive portion of the operating system then dynamically determines the assignment of the CPU to this program, at which point it may execute. The course of the execution will then involve application program instructions that lie outside of the set of programs making up the operating system. On the other hand, since the function of the executive portion is to distribute the I/O facilities of the computer system to the application programs, it is evidently necessary that the execution of an application program pass over to the execution of the executive programs in order for it to accomplish this function. In transaction terms we will say that the transaction representing the execution of the application program is passed into the operating system, where it is then manipulated by the transaction representing the execution of the executive program.

There is a physical characteristic of virtually all of the modern computing systems that corresponds directly to the conceptual segregation of application and operating system programs described above. This is known as the "privileged instruction mode." A computing system with this capability is said to be operating in one of two modes, or states. These are the application mode and the operating system mode. The current mode for the system is determined by a hardware switch that may be set or reset by instructions in the instruction repertoire. Privileged instructions are then defined as those instructions of the instruction repertoire that may be executed only when the computer system is in the operating system mode. The set of instructions for positioning files on peripheral devices and initiating data transfers between those devices and core memory is an example. Thus, in order to actually execute an I/O activity, it is necessary for the CPU to pass from execution of instructions in the application program to execution of instructions within the operating system. In particular, it must pass to execution of those instructions in the executive portion that activate the required peripheral equipments.

Interrupts

A computer program consists of instructions that carry out certain testing and data manipulation operations, and other instructions that conditionally and unconditionally transfer the execution to specified points in the program. This is the dynamic sequence of execution of the computer program. Any interruption of the dynamic sequence that transfers the execution to instructions in a program other than the one being executed at the time of interruption is referred to as an "interrupt."

The actual interrupt mechanism differs from computer to computer, but they share in common a logical approach. Thus, at the moment of interrupt, the system mode is changed to the operating system mode. The location of the position in the interrupted program at which the interruption occurred is noted, and the next instruction to be executed is taken from a fixed location in the core memory. It can be seen then that an interrupt literally forces the execution to pass from the application program into the operating system by a change of mode. In addition, the place at which the interruption occurred in the application program is made available for storage so that at some later point the execution of this interrupted program may be resumed from the point of interruption. Finally, the next instruction is taken from a fixed location within the core memory, thus allowing the next logical actions of the computer system to be determined by instructions starting in that location. Since the mode of the system has been changed, execution now is within the operating system, so that this instruction will be the first instruction within the operating system to be executed on interrupt.

There are three categories of interrupt, each of which is described below. Within each of these categories, it may also be necessary to distinguish between particular interrupt sources. Therefore, the logical functions to be accomplished by execution of operating system programs on interrupt entry will ordinarily start with "interrupt processing," the purposes of which is to determine the category and identity of the particular interrupt.

The three interrupt categories are "alert," "forced entry," and "generated." The alert interrupts are created by activating external switches that signify external conditions to the operating system. Thus for example, a system with an operator console will generally have an alert interrupt button that will allow the operator to gain the computer system's attention. The identity of an interrupt within the alert class distinguishes, for example, between an interrupt that is associated with the operator console, and an interrupt that would denote, say, the mounting and activation of a tape transport.

Interrupts falling into the forced entry class occur as the result of instruction executions in the application mode that can only be operated by privileged instructions in the operating system mode. For example, the READ "macro" in an application program creates a forced entry to the operating system where the I/O programs of the executive will actually carry out the required device manipulations and data transfer. Interrupts within the forced entry class must be identified in order to distinguish, for example, between a forced entry for the purpose of READ and a forced entry for the purpose of WRITE.

Interrupts may occur at the present time that were generated at an earlier time by the execution of certain programs. These are the generated interrupt class, the most familiar example for which is the I/O termination interrupts occurring on the completion of a peripheral device activity. Identification of interrupts within this class is necessary to determine the specific peripheral device whose termination of activity has caused the interrupt.

It is evident from the foregoing that the notion of privileged instructions in the modern day computer requires that application and operating system programs be logically segregated. This is achieved via dual operation modes, with the users given access to the operating system via forced entry interrupts only. In the chapters that follow we shall develop a notational form that is suited to representing this segregation of the application programs from the operating system.

Memory Distribution and Protection

A word should be said at this point concerning the segregation of application programs from one another. In general, the several concurrent users of a computing system are individually unaware of the presence of other application programs. In particular, their coresidence in the core memory makes it mandatory that the memory locations assigned to individual programs be completely under the control of the operating system. The operating system thus provides a central repository for all information concerning the assignment of core memory locations to the currently resident application programs, accomplishing this in the form of a so-called "memory map." As a consequence of designating the locations currently assigned to programs, the operating system is therefore aware of the unassigned, or available, locations and operates its "allocator" to provide memory space for new application programs seeking access to the system.

Certain computers have a "memory protection" hardware capability. This may briefly be described as a mechanism for restraining the operations of a given program to its assigned core memory locations. Since the allocation of memory space must necessarily be among the functions of the operating system, the protection of core memory will obviously be a function that also resides in the operating system. Thus, memory protection may be thought of as a means for isolating, or segregating independent application programs from one another, as well as from the operating system.

CHAPTER 3

SOME GENERAL CONSIDERATIONS

CONSIDER A COMPUTER system that has a large collection of peripheral devices available to it via a number of I/O channels. Suppose further that this system has a very large core memory and an extremely fast central processing unit. For the sake of example, let us consider specific quantities; suppose that there are two sets of eight tape units with an I/O channel for each set. In addition, assume a random access device on its own channel, plus a printer and card reader on separate channels. Let us further suppose that the memory makes 96*K* instruction locations available, and, after the storage allocated to the operating system, provides room for, say, 90*K* instructions. Finally, let us suppose a two microsecond average execution time for the CPU with a memory cycle time sufficiently fast to accommodate this speed.

In the first place, it should be clear that for the average user of such a large scale system most of the available capacity will go begging, since it would take a large program indeed to use all sixteen tape units as well as all available channel time to the random access device. Furthermore, it is not often that a program is as large as 90*K* instructions, and more than likely will not even approximate half that amount. Finally, a program using an extensive array of peripheral devices very likely will be characterized by a high frequency of instructions that call for I/O relative to these devices. Therefore, the computing time between I/O operations can be expected to be short. It follows then that with a two microsecond average execution time, and considering the speed of even the fastest peripheral devices available on the market today, one would certainly expect the CPU to be idle for a significant fraction of the time.

Even in simpler situations, where the entire computing facility is given over to execution of a single program at a time and which only uses a few of the available peripheral devices, we are again faced with idle system facilities. This extends easily to the unused portion of the computer system memory that lies idle during the execution of a single program in control of the entire computer system.

Again, even for those programs which are able to achieve a successful balanced buffering, unless they are involved with all of the peripheral devices, the throughput on the unusued devices is zero. In fact, even for programs using all peripheral devices, or a suitably large fraction of those available, it is entirely questionable whether any sufficient degree of I/O balancing is possible, given the tremendous disparity in operating speeds between the peripheral device rates and a two miscrosecond CPU.

The purpose of multiprogramming, therefore, is to attempt to distribute the facilities of the computer system, i.e. its peripheral devices, its CPU, and its available core memory to several programs. These programs exist in the system concurrently, using the memory and the set of peripheral devices simultaneously, and the CPU facility of the system sequentially.

Time-slicing

Multiprogramming is a name applied to a variety of techniques aimed at introducing more than one program into a computer for concurrent operation. The chief goal of early attempts at multiprogramming was to allow more than one user access to the computing system at a given time. A secondary goal has been to effect an increase in the throughput of the computing system. One approach to achieving the goal of multiuser capability is "time-slice" multiprogramming.

Each program in the system that is available for execution is given control of the entire computing facility for a designated amount of time, or time-slice. At the end of this time-slice period, control of the system's facilities is taken away from the *current operating program* and given next to some other program. Hence, if the next program to be given control is resident in the core memory, the operations involved are relatively simple and straightforward. On the other hand, if the program is resident on a peripheral device, such as a random access memory, then the necessary operations require the operating system to make room in the core memory (usually done by rolling out some other program) and to read in the required program.

In this approach to multiprogramming, the operating system's function is to control the execution of a selected program resident in memory for some preset length of time. When this program's time allotment, or slice, expires, it is interrupted; information concerning the program's status is stored for a subsequent reselection of the program; finally, another program is selected for execution. This technique results in operations that remain essentially "sequential." The only basic difference between this and a traditional sequential processor is that instead of processing complete programs in sequence, parts of programs are processed in sequence. The individual program's overall time in memory is increased, system throughput is not improved, and the only genuine gain of such an approach to multiprogramming occurs in the case of users at remote consoles where several users may concurrently carry out necessary communications with their programs.

Time-slice multiprogramming does improve the efficiency of the computer system in one dimension however, namely, the degree of utilization of the core memory. This is due to the fact that for a large enough core memory and suitably sized user programs, several of them may concurrently be resident in the core memory. On the other hand, time-slice multiprogramming offers no improvements relative to the utilization of the CPU or peripheral device facilities of the system. In the first place, since there is only one CPU and it is given over to the user programs one at a time, its application is strictly sequential relative to the several programs waiting for it. A similar remark must be made with respect to the peripheral devices. For although these devices are assigned in parallel, they are not operated simultaneously. This is due to the fact that the time-slice technique gives control to just one of the waiting programs at a time. Therefore, when a given program becomes the current operating program, the subset of peripheral devices assigned for its execution offer the only possibility for simultaneous activity. Since the other programs are not executing, their associated peripheral devices will not be operating.

It is therefore clear from the above discussion that time-slice multiprogramming offers little in the way of improved computer system throughput and can have only a small effect on a user's expected turnaround time. In fact, the only place where this type of multiprogramming has any effect and consequent value is when it is associated with a so-called "time-sharing" environment. This is because in such an environment there is the ever present need to set programs aside while awaiting a response from a remote terminal user. If many users are to have access to the system concurrently, time-slice multiprogramming sees to it that each of the user's actions receives computer system attention in a series of time quanta.

In view of the foregoing, we seek other techniques for multiprogramming that improve the efficiency of use of both the CPU and peripheral device facilities, as well as that of memory. In order to improve the utilization of the CPU our objective is to have it executing instructions in any program that is not delayed by an I/O operation. On the other hand, the objectives to be achieved with respect to the peripheral devices of the system by virtue of multiprogramming are somewhat more complex. In general, however, we shall say that we seek to maximize the simultaneity of device operations and at the same time to maximize throughput on each device. As will be pointed out in what follows, these two objectives are not always compatible.

I/O Demand Multiprogramming

An alternative approach to time-slice multiprogramming is a technique that we shall refer to as I/O demand multiprogramming. Simply stated, this method employs variable time-slices of unpredictable length, each defined by the interval between successive I/O termination interrupts. Whenever a peripheral device has completed an I/O, the operating system undertakes to initiate another immediately, if such a requirement exists at the time. Thus, the I/O operations, or more explicitly the I/O terminations, drive the system in the sense that their occurrences determine the change of control, or selection, of a new current operating program. Hence, the system is oriented toward meeting the I/O demands made on it and distributing and redistributing the CPU facility on the basis of this I/O demand and its associated interrupts. It should be noted that this is somewhat different than the situation obtained in the case of time-slice. There, the primary objective was distribution of the CPU facility to a program. A consequence of the selection of a program was the I/O activity it generated over its alloted time-slice.

One of the important virtues of the I/O demand approach is that it tends to provide for a more uniform distribution of the CPU among the set of programs seeking it, and it selects the next program at the time when an I/O termination has occurred so that there exists at least one program that is available for execution, and hence utilizes the CPU. More importantly however, I/O demand multiprogramming provides the opportunity for a much more rapid distribution of the CPU to all programs and thereby broadens the opportunity to initiate diverse I/O activities.

It should now be clear that the real difference between time-slice and I/O demand multiprogramming is a question of control. In the time-slice approach, the user program is given control over all system facilities that have been assigned to it. A change of current operating program occurs only when the time-slice has been exhausted, or if the user program itself realizes that it has hit a temporary stall awaiting completion of data transfers. In the latter case, it is necessary for this program to relinguish its control of the CPU to the operating system. The situation for I/O demand multiprogramming is just the opposite. In this case, the operating system retains control over the peripheral devices, giving the user program access to the CPU facility only. I/O activities are monitored by the operating system so that whenever a data transfer condition causes the user program to be delayed, it is forced to give up control. It is by this means that a much higher degree of peripheral device simultaneity can be achieved.

As mentioned earlier, however, one of the objectives that we seek relative to the peripheral devices is to maximize their individual throughput. Also mentioned was the fact that the maximization of both throughput and device simultaneity are not always compatible. We therefore next discuss two different types of I/O demand multiprogramming, each of which tends to enhance one of these two objectives at a possible expense to the other.

Unbuffered I/O Demand

The simplest and most straightforward system to consider is the one in which all user program I/O operations are carried out on a strictly unbuffered basis. This means that whenever a current operating program causes a data transfer activity between a peripheral device and the core memory as a consequence of its execution of I/O instructions, the program is deferred from further execution until the corresponding data transfer operation has been completed. This completion is indicated by the occurrence of an I/O termination interrupt. When a program initiates such an I/O activity, it is necessarily the current operating program, and to carry out an I/O it must transfer to the operating system. Here the requested I/O function is initiated relative to the designated device if that is possible, or an identifier for that program is placed in a queue associated with the required device if it is busy. In this fashion the program is deferred from further execution until the completion of the data transfer and satisfaction of the I/O request. The next step for the operating system is to select a new current operating program and to resume its execution.

Thus, each I/O call causes a redistribution of the CPU facility, and it is therefore clear that the widest possible collection of peripheral devices will be activated and operated, giving the greatest degree of device simultaneity by virtue of achieving the widest possible distribution of the CPU among the members of the multiprogram set. On the other hand, it is also clear that on a per device basis this approach may provide a minimum throughput. This is most likely the case for sequential devices such as magnetic tape, or punched cards, and may be true for certain random access devices. For magnetic tape, the unit is usually assigned to one and only one program. Let us suppose that the tape is for, say, input. This means that each call for the next record that empties the input block and initiates a data transfer defers further execution until the transfer from the tape is completed. Following this, an amount of time will then elapse until this program is next selected as the current operating program. In this case, there will be an attendant throughput loss if start-stop time for the tape is a significant factor in the timing of the overall data transfer operation.

Consider now a random access device, such as a disk, having a single movable access arm. Sequential reads from a file on the disk by a given program may very well take advantage of the current arm position in attempting to minimize seek time and maximize throughput for this device relative to the particular program. On the other hand, several programs using such a disk concurrently and in the context of an unbuffered I/O demand environment, may, by virtue of the diversity of locations sought on the disk, develop a throughput rate which is minimal. It is clear, however, that this is not a problem for head-per-track disks, or fixed-head drums. Here, seek time is effectively the latency time that must be suffered in all events so that switching from program to program, and the consequent switching from access area to access area on such a random access device, has virtually no effect on the throughput.

Buffered I/O Demand

As a general description, buffering is a technique that allows the user to initiate an I/O activity and then to continue his execution in parallel with the data transfer operation. This is, of course, accomplished in an unbuffered multiprogramming environment as well by some other program, so long as there is some other program in the multiprogram set seeking access to the CPU facility. But in the present case we are interested in allowing the user causing the I/O activity to continue in parallel with the activity his program has created. The advantage to this approach is possibly twofold. In the first place, the probability that a situation will arise where the CPU facility is available, with no user program waiting to employ it, will be reduced appreciably. In the second place, for certain peripheral devices the buffering capability may be necessary in order to maximize throughput on them. This is particularly the case with movable arm disks; certain presentation data devices, such as the high speed printer; and other sequential devices as noted earlier.

On the other hand, there is a potential attendant difficulty to be associated with a buffered multiprogramming environment. As mentioned earlier, the objective of the operating system in trying to maximize throughput system-wide is to attempt to maximize throughput on each of the peripheral devices and to maximize the simultaneity of their use. The unbuffered multiprogramming environment tends to maximize the simultaneity of peripheral device use, but at the same time tends to reduce the throughput on the individual devices. In the present case, the user program operating in an environment that allows buffering has control not only of the CPU facility, but simultaneously of some subset of the peripheral devices assigned to it as well. Therefore, the maximum degree of peripheral device simultaneity is restricted to that which this current operating program can achieve among the peripheral devices assigned to it. Hence, the buffering environment offers the possibility of loss of general I/O throughput due to a lowering of the degree of simultaneity that can be achieved among the peripheral devices.

Remarks

From the above discussions it is by no means settled that either buffered or unbuffered operation of user programs in an I/O demand environment is to be preferred. In fact, the choice is apparently dependent upon performance objectives to be achieved. Thus, for example, if the performance objective is to maximize the throughput of the system, then it might well be that the largest number of programs, all running unbuffered, will gain this result. On the other hand, if minimum turnaround time for one or several users represented by programs in the system is desired, then the buffered approach seems more likely to achieve success.

But it should be clearly understood that the choice is not so neatly delineated as the above brief paragraph might suggest. If one seeks to maximize throughput (at the possible expense of individual turnaround time) by requiring all programs in the system to execute unbuffered I/O, it may be that the consequent throughput loss per device is so extreme that an impossibly poor overall performance results. By the same token, if turnaround time is to be improved for a selected subset of the programs currently running in the system, then it must be at the expense of turnaround time for other programs of the system. Furthermore, there are questions as to the degree of buffering to be supplied for a buffering program, and finally, questions as to the cost required to operate these buffering mechanisms.

Obviously the choice is not a simple one, and, in any event, has its answer dependent upon the specific computing environment against which it is applied. Our purpose in this work, however, is to isolate, elucidate, and elaborate so that we can here address such questions in only the most general and theoretical terms. Therefore, in the next chapter we consider the simpler problem, from the operating system point of view, of user programs running in an unbuffered I/O demand environment. In subsequent chapters, we more carefully analyze the nature of buffering, and then consider in some detail operating systems that provide for it.

CHAPTER 4

UNBUFFERED I/O DEMAND EXECUTIVE

Introduction

IN CHAPTER 3, motives were given for considering the multiprogramming environment wherein each worker program is allowed to only execute unbuffered I/O operations. The result of this approach is a tendency to maximize the degree of device simultaneity achieved over all peripheral devices. More importantly, the multiprogram executive (MPX) is completely determined by such a condition. Therefore in this chapter, we develop the MPX for unbuffered I/O demand multiprogramming, describing it via conventional techniques. In Chapters 5, we retrace this development in terms of a complete "transaction analysis" of MPX. With this accomplished, Chapter 7 can be devoted to the analysis of a simple, but surprisingly powerful, multiprogramming system, the MPX for which is the subject of the present discussion.

General

The nucleus of the operating system is the multiprogramming executive (MPX), and it is this basic element which will determine the effectiveness of the overall system. We shall generally refer to user or application programs as "worker programs," or more simply as "workers." The use of this term then implies that the program so designated is not considered as part of the operating system. The set of programs under control of the executive will be referred to as the multiprogram set." The chief goal of the executive developed in this chapter is to selectively control the concurrent operation of the set of worker programs in the multiprogram set by controlling its I/O operations in a manner that will achieve maximum simultaneity of I/O operations for all of them. The selection of programs for execution will be on a strict priority basis.

It is obvious that first consideration must be given to the maintenance of information regarding the state of each program in the set at any given time with regard to its I/O operations. We shall therefore start by considering the exact nature of the various states in which an unbuffered worker program can exist.

Program States

First, assume that a worker program currently executing in the main frame has just made an I/O reference to a device on a channel, and that one or both of these is busy. This program is now said to be in the state of awaiting the initiation of an I/O operation. Since it is unbuffered, this program is not available for execution, nor has it an I/O activity currently in operation.

Second, consider the current operating worker program that has made an I/O reference to a device on a channel where both of these are available, and the I/O operation is initiated. The program is then considered to be in the state of awaiting the completion of this I/O operation. Again, because the program is executing unbuffered I/O's, in this state it is not available for further execution.

Third, a worker program which is neither waiting for the initiation of an I/O operation or the termination of an I/O operation can be considered to be in the state of being available for execution. In addition, we shall say that the current operating program is in this state as well.

A review of these states will show that these three conditions are all-inclusive and mutually exclusive for any program in the multiprogram set. That is, each program in the multiprogram set can satisfy one and only one of these conditions:

1) awaiting the initiation of an I/O operation
2) awaiting termination of an I/O operation
3) neither of the above; ergo, available for execution, or the current operating program.

It should be clear that if a program is in state 3, it will at some point be selected as the current operating program. Its execution may then be expected to lead to input/output references requiring a data transfer between a peripheral device and core memory. When this occurs, the program will move out of state 3 and into either state 1 or state 2 depending on the availability of the necessary components for inaugurating the required data transfer. Thus, if the data transfer activity cannot be instituted at this time, the program will pass into state 1 and will remain in that state until termination of other I/O activity in the system makes the necessary equipments available. At that point, the data transfer may be initiated for this program and it can then be moved from state 1 into state 2. On the other hand, if at the time of the I/O reference during the execution of the program while in state 3, the data transfer operation was able to be immediately initiated, then the program would make a transition from state 3 directly into state 2. In any event, however a program arrives in state 2, it will remain there until the data transfer initiated for it has been completed, after which the program can be moved from state 2 back into state 3. This movement among the three program states is summarized in the transition diagram shown below.

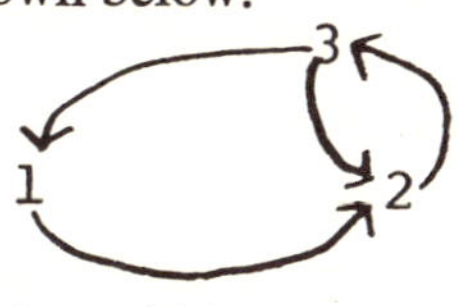

In order to maintain, within the executive, the condition or state of each program within the multiprogram set, three lists are required which we shall temporarily call the available list (AL), the initiation list (IL), and the reference list (RL). A program (identified by an "ID") on AL is available for execution (state 3). A program on IL is awaiting the initiation of an I/O operation (state 1), and a program on RL is awaiting the termination of an I/O operation that has already been initiated (state 2).

At this point, it is evident that the multiprogramming executive must serve as an interface between the programs of the multiprogram set and the operating system I/O package. That is, each call for input or output must be directed to the multiprogramming executive. The executive will pass these calls to the I/O package as directed by priority and device and channel availabilities. I/O termination interrupts will be routed through the I/O package. With MPX thus located in the system, some of the possibilities and methods for the control of program states can be considered. We begin with an example showing the conditions under which changes of state occur.

Figure 1 (top row, *A*) indicates that programs 1, 3, and 5 are available for execution, that programs 2 and 4 are awaiting initiation of an I/O operation, and that programs 6, 7, and 8 are awaiting the termination of I/O operations. Program 9 is the program currently being executed. The first question to be asked is how did the executive know that programs 2 and 4 could not have their I/O requests initiated at the time they made their respective calls on the executive, and how is the executive going to know when the I/O operations are terminated for programs 6, 7, and 8? The answer is that Fig. 1, *A* does not provide sufficient information in the list structures to answer these questions. They can be quite simply answered, however, by a small modification to list RL. Assume that the computer being used has eight channels. The length of RL can then be fixed at eight words, with each word on the list corresponding to one of the channels (Fig. 1, *B*). Whenever an I/O operation is requested, this call on the executive will put the ID for the requesting program into the corresponding channel word of RL if that word is zero at the time of the request. The executive will then initiate the I/O operation requested. The presence of the ID for the requesting program in the channel word of RL will now indicate that the channel is busy. This is what occurred in

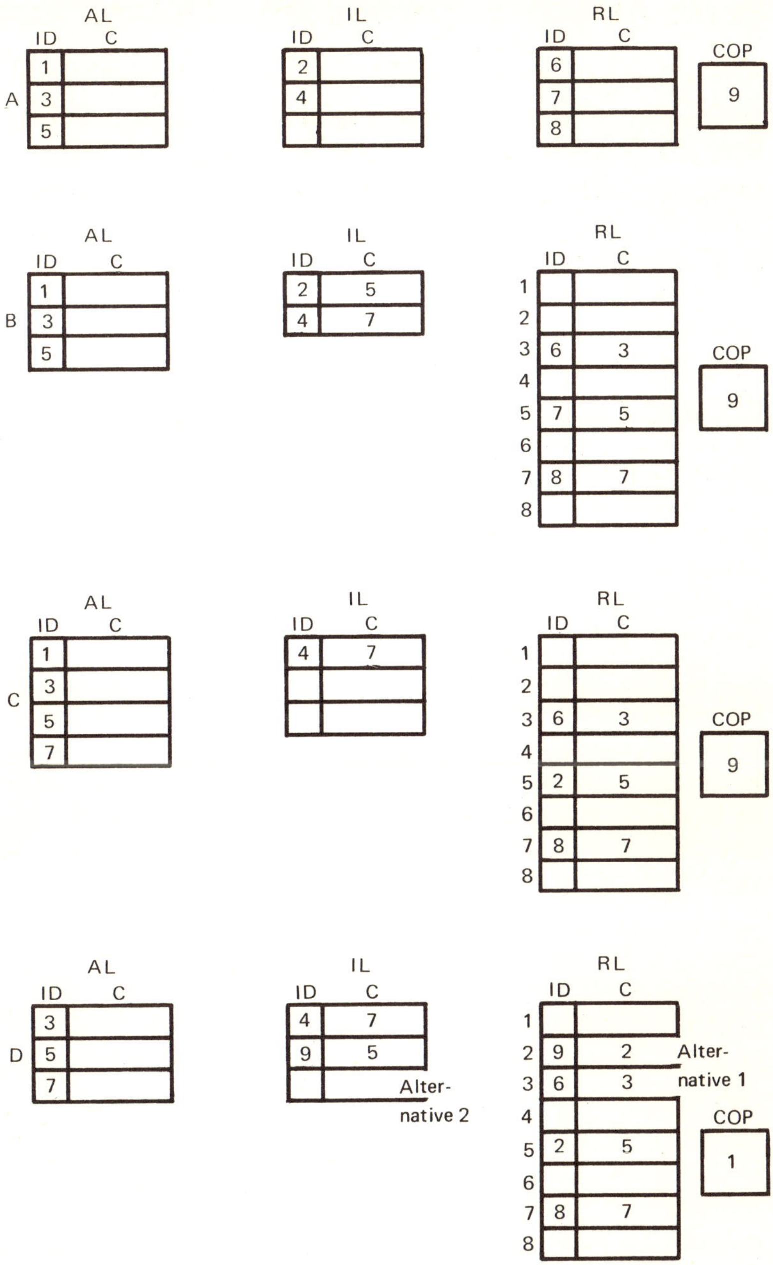

Fig. 1. Development of Executive Control

the case of I/O calls from programs 6, 7, and 8. In the case of the I/O calls from programs 2 and 4, the presence of ID's in the reference list indicated that channels 5 and 7 (which they respectively required) were already busy performing I/O functions for programs 7 and 8. MPX therefore put the ID's for programs 2 and 4 on the initiation list along with the channels which they require for their I/O operations.

At this point, assume in Fig. 1, *B* that during the execution of the current operating program, 9, an I/O termination interrupt indicates that the operation on channel 5 is completed. The executive will remove the ID for program 7 from word five of the RL, place it in the available list (AL) and zero word five of RL. It then examines the initiation list for a program that requires channel 5. In this case, the I/O operation for program 2 can now be initiated because its required channel is free. Hence, the ID for program 2 is moved into the fifth word of the reference list, and the I/O operation is initiated. Finally, control is returned to the current operating program, 9, leaving the system in the state indicated in Fig. 1, *C*.

With the conditions as shown in Fig. 1, *C*, assume next that the current operating program, 9, has called MPX with an I/O request. If the channel required for the I/O operation is channel 2, which, in this example, is available, the I/O operation will be initiated, and the ID for program 9 will be placed in the second word of RL (Fig. 1, *D*, alternative 1). If the I/O request required channel 5 for execution however, the ID for program 9 would be placed on the initiation list (Fig. 1, *D*, alternative 2). In either event, program 9 is no longer available for execution, and its ID is removed from AL. The executive now selects, from the remaining programs on AL, a new current operating program. This selection results in program 1 as COP, leaving the new state of the system as shown in Fig. 1, *D*, alternative 1 or alternative 2 obtaining.

Priority

From the above example it is apparent that, although MPX has maintained control of the state of the various worker programs in the multiprogram set, it has demonstrated no control whatsoever over the varying priorities which might exist among the programs of the set. This problem is readily solved by changing two of the lists to queues. Instead of an available list, AL, MPX will maintain an available queue, to be referred to as AQ. The AQ will contain the ID's of programs available for execution in priority sequence. Similarly, the initiation list, IL, will become the initiation queue, IQ. As in the case of AQ, ID's are maintained in IQ in accordance with their priority on a per channel basis. An examination of Fig. 2 will demonstrate the priority control that can be maintained in the selection of programs for execution, and in the initiation of their I/O operations. Figure 2, *A* indicates the initial configuration of the lists and queues for each of the following cases, with the program priority indicated in parentheses.

Assume that an I/O termination interrupt indicates that channel 7 has completed its activity. This means that the I/O operation for program 8 has been completed so that program 8 may now be considered as being available for execution. The executive will remove the ID for program 8 from the reference list, zero word seven of the list to indicate the channel's availability, and insert the ID for program 8, by priority, into AQ. Thus, program 8 has made the transition from state 2 to state 3. The executive then examines the initiation queue, where it finds two programs awaiting the initiation of I/O operations on channel 7. Because of its priority in the queue, program 4 will be selected and its I/O initiated. As previously described, the ID for program 4 is moved to the reference list by channel (i.e. word seven), completing a transition from state 1 to state 2. MPX next examines the available queue, which now shows that program 1 is the highest priority program available for execution, replacing the interrupted current operating program, program 9, the ID for which is returned in priority order to AQ since it remains in state 3. Program 1 is thus selected as the new current operating program. This sequence of operations results in the transition from Fig. 2, *A* to Fig. 2, *B*.

Figure 2, *C* refers to the case where the current operating program has requested the initiation of an I/O operation. Suppose that the channel required for the operation is channel three

A

AQ

ID	C	P
1		(Ø)
3		(3)
5		(4)

IQ

ID	C	P
2	5	(2)
4	7	(6)
1Ø	7	(9)

RL

	ID	C	P
1			
2			
3	6	3	(3)
4			
5	7	5	(7)
6			
7	8	7	(1)
8			

COP

9 P = 8

B

AQ

ID	C	P
8		(1)
3		(3)
5		(4)
9		(8)

IQ

ID	C	P
2	5	(2)
1Ø	7	(9)

RL

	ID	C	P
1			
2			
3	6	3	(3)
4			
5	7	5	(7)
6			
7	4	7	(6)
8			

COP

1 P = Ø

C

AQ

ID	C	P
3		(3)
5		(4)

IQ

ID	C	P	
2	5	(2)	
9	3	(8)	Alter-
1Ø	7	(9)	native
			1

RL

	ID	C	P	
1	9	1	(8)	
2				
3	6	3	(3)	Alter-
4				native
5	7	5	(7)	2
6				
7	4	7	(6)	
8				

COP

1 P = Ø

Fig. 2. Development of Executive Control

(indicated in the center column of IQ). Since it is not available (alternative 1), the executive will insert the ID for program 9 into the initiation queue according to its priority. The ID for program 9 is removed from the available queue and program 1 is selected from its priority position at the top of AQ as the new current operating program. Thus, in this example, the current operating program has made the transition from state 3 to state 1.

On the other hand, suppose that program 9 requires channel 1. From the reference list it can be seen that word one is zero, implying that channel 1 is available. In this case (alternative 2), the ID for program 9 is moved to word one of the reference list, removing it from AQ. The I/O is initiated, and as before, program 1 is selected to be the current operating program.

It is evident that these two queues, and a list representing the available channels of the system, are sufficient for maintaining the program states of unbuffered worker programs, and for the ensuing selection of programs for execution and initiation of I/O calls on a priority basis. A detailed discussion of the controller algorithm and the exact functioning of the multiprogramming executive is now in order. The four flow charts in Figs. 3, 4, 5, and 6 delineate the complete multiprogramming executive for the handling of I/O calls to the executive, I/O termination interrupts, and program terminations.

I/O Calls

With reference to Fig. 3, consider the case where a worker program in the set has established a calling sequence for an I/O operation and has made an entry to the executive. Starting in box 1 in the I/O request routine, further I/O termination interrupts are disabled. This is necessary because the executive will shortly be modifying the lists and queues relating to the state of the program involved. Any time an I/O request is being executed, an I/O termination interrupt cannot be processed since this routine will also attempt to modify the same lists and queues. Generally speaking, once modification of any of the lists and/or queues of the executive is started, I/O interrupts may not be allowed until the modification is complete.

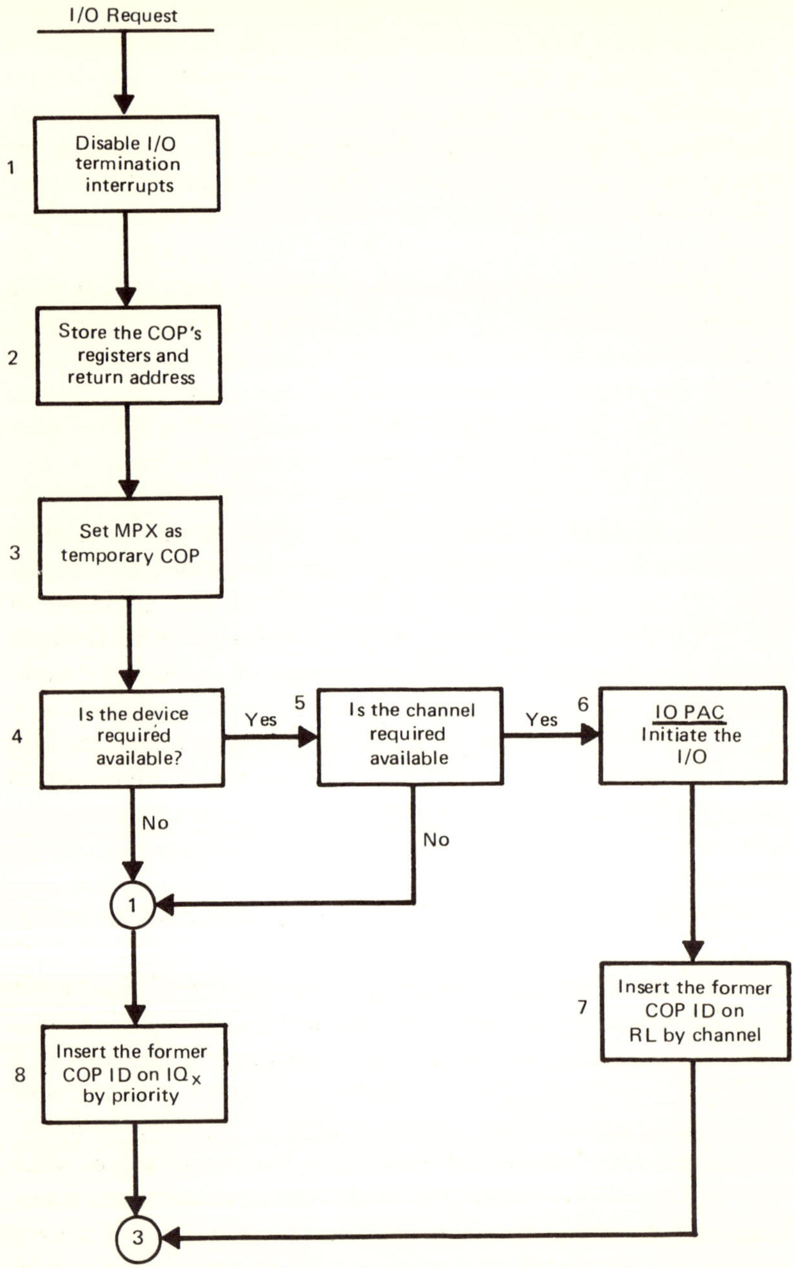

Fig. 3. Multiprogramming Executive, Flow Chart 1

In box 2 of the I/O request routine, the executive will store in memory the contents of the registers, indexes, etc., which were being utilized by the current operating program at the time it made the I/O call. The executive will also store the address to which it should return when this program is again selected for execution. Next, the multiprogramming executive itself becomes the current operating program. This allows the executive to be interrupted for any reason other than I/O termination, so that these interrupts can be handled immediately, with control ultimately returning to the executive at the point of interruption. (Note that interrupts other than I/O termination do not generally require manipulation of any of the control lists or queues of the executive.) Now a check is made to see if the device required by this I/O call is available (box 4). Examples of devices that might not be available at a given time, despite the fact that the channel required is available, would be a magnetic tape in a rewind condition, a random access device executing a seek instruction, etc.

Given the device, a test is then made to determine whether the channel required for the I/O operation is available (box 5), and if either the device or the channel is unavailable, a transfer is made to connector one. Since this I/O operation cannot be initiated, the ID for the worker program that made the call will be placed on the initiation queue for the channel involved according to its priority (box 8).

Returning now to the tests at boxes 4 and 5 of this flow chart, assume that the device and the channel required for the I/O operation are both available. In this case (box 6), a subroutine transfer is made to the I/O package where the requesting program's calling sequence is interpreted and the I/O operation initiated. The executive places the ID of the requesting program on the reference list (by channel) indicating that the channel is unavailable until termination of this I/O operation. Control is then transferred to connector three.

At connector three, depending upon device and channel availability, the I/O operation has either been initiated with the program's ID going to the reference list to indicate this, or the I/O operation has not been initiated and the ID for the program

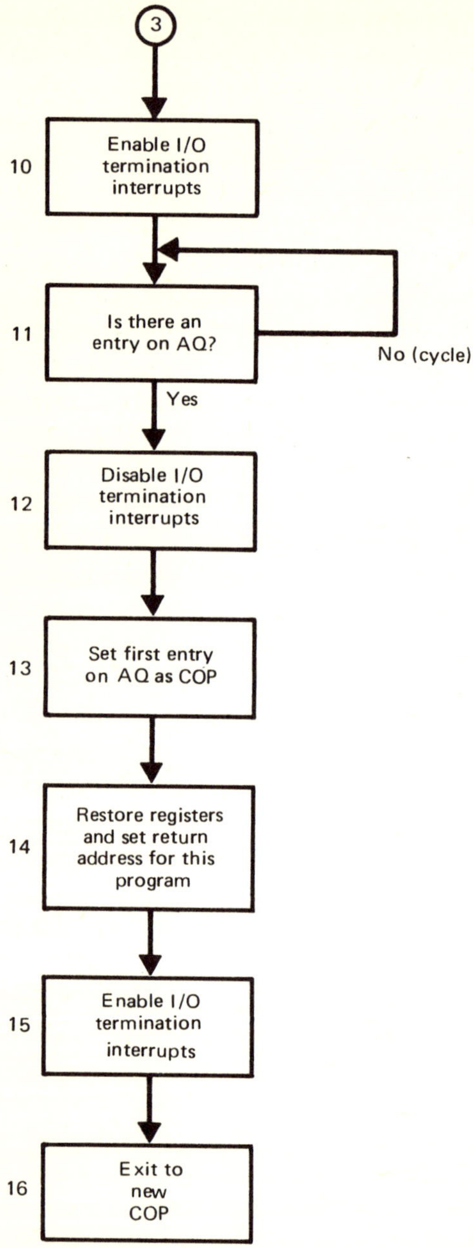

Fig. 4. Multiprogramming Executive, Flow Chart 2

has been placed on the initiation queue for the channel required. In either case, a transition from state 3 has been made to either state 2 or state 1. The next step is for MPX to select a program from among those in state 3 to become the next current operating program. This is accomplished by the operations beginning at connector three.

At connector three of Fig. 4, I/O interrupts are enabled and a test made (box 11) to determine if there is an entry on the available queue. If all of the programs of the set are either awaiting I/O initiation (state 1) or I/O termination (state 2), the executive simply loops through this test until an I/O termination occurs. This I/O termination will make a program available for execution, and the I/O termination interrupt (now enabled) will ultimately lead back to connector three where the test at box 11 will pass. In the normal case, there will be an entry on the available queue, and the executive disables the I/O termination interrupts (box 12) selecting the first (highest priority) entry in the available queue as the current operating program (box 13). Finally (box 14), the executive will restore the registers and indexes to the conditions that existed when this program last made an I/O request or was interrupted by an I/O termination. The exit address (box 16) is set to correspond to the return address that was stored for this program, the I/O termination interrupts are again enabled, and control is transferred to the new current operating program.

I/O Termination

Assume that a worker program is executing, and an I/O termination interrupt occurs indicating that an I/O operation on the channel to which the interrupt relates has been completed. Upon interpretation of this interrupt, control is transferred to the I/O interrupt entry of the executive as shown in Fig. 5. Starting at box 17, the initial procedure is the same as that followed on an I/O call. The executive disables any further I/O termination interrupts and stores the registers and indexes for the current operating program and the address to which the executive will return control when this program is next selected for execution. MPX is made the current operating program and, at box 20, the

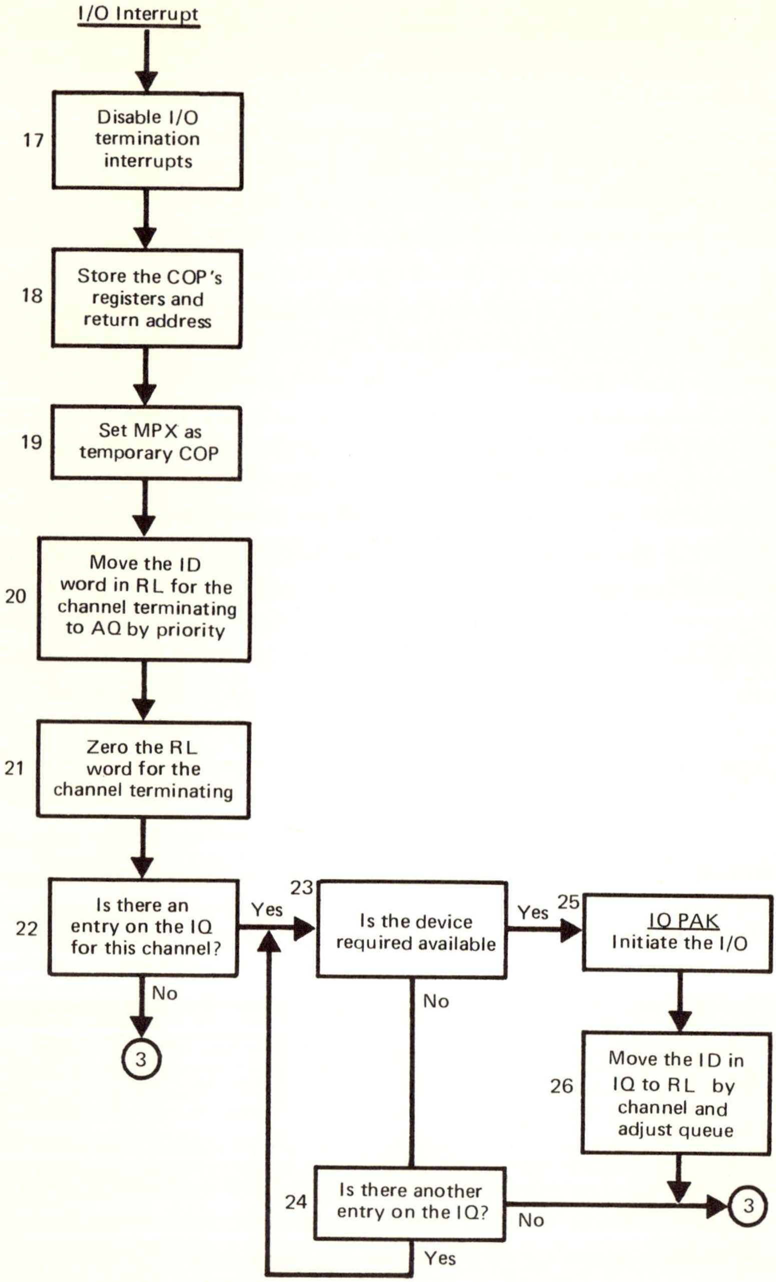

Fig. 5. Multiprogramming Executive, Flow Chart 3

ID in the reference list corresponding to the channel on which the termination occurred is placed on the available queue according to its priority. At box 21 that word of the reference list is zero filled, indicating that the channel is again available for I/O.

Since the channel is available, a test is made (box 22) to see if there is an entry on the initiation queue for this channel. If not, control is transferred to connector three, where, as previously described, the selection of a new current operating program is made. If there are entries on the initiation queue for the available channel, a test is made to determine if the device required is available (box 23) and if not, a test is made at box 24 to determine if there are any more entries on the initiation queue for this channel. If there are, the next entry on the queue will be tested. This loop will test all entries to determine if one of them can be initiated. When a call is found on the initiation queue for the available channel whose required device is also available, a subroutine transfer is made to the I/O package to initiate the operation, and, at box 26, the program ID relating to the call in question is removed from the initiation queue and inserted in that word of the reference list corresponding to the channel required.

In either event, once an I/O operation has been initiated on the channel, or it has been determined that there are no I/O operations that can be initiated at this time, control is transferred to connector three for selection of a new current operating program.

It is these two events, I/O request and I/O termination, that trigger the complete cycle of a given program through the three states in which it can exist in the multiprogram set. Note that whenever a program makes an I/O request, an attempt is made to initiate its I/O operation immediately. If this is not possible, it is held on an initiation queue and initiated immediately after the device and channel required become available, assuming that its priority position relative to other programs of the set so warrants. In the case of an I/O request, an effort is made to immediately initiate the I/O operation because the call comes from what is obviously the highest priority program available for execution. Any higher priority programs are either awaiting the termination of an I/O operation or are on a queue awaiting I/O initiation.

Program Termination

The third entry to the multiprogramming executive is the entry made by a worker program when it has completed its task in the computer. This entry has no effect on program states, except for the condition of the terminating program, and does not involve any manipulation or changes in the lists and queues that control the state of the programs in the multiprogram set. The flow chart in Fig. 6 indicates the general course of action followed by the executive on a call to the program termination entry. As before, the I/O termination interrupts are disabled, and MPX is made the temporary current operating program. At box 3, the program's termination is effectively indicated by removing its ID from the available queue, thereby making this program no longer available for selection. Since AQ is the only queue retaining this ID, its removal wipes out all memory of its presence in the multiprogram set.

The remainder of this flow chart indicates the tasks of the executive with relation to the terminating program. Briefly, at box 4, devices that had been assigned upon initiation of the program are returned to an available status for reassignment to other programs coming into the system. At box 5, the memory that has been occupied by the terminating program is returned to an available status for reassignment. Following this, control is transferred to connector three in the multiprogramming executive for selection to a new current operating program.

Nothing is done with regard to I/O operations because all possible I/O's were initiated in the last course through the executive which led to the selection of this terminating program for execution. Therefore, since this program has not made an I/O call, and since an I/O interrupt has not occurred, there has been no change in the status of the I/O activities of the system.

General Remarks

The executive developed in this chapter is derived directly from the assumption that all I/O activity created by worker pro-

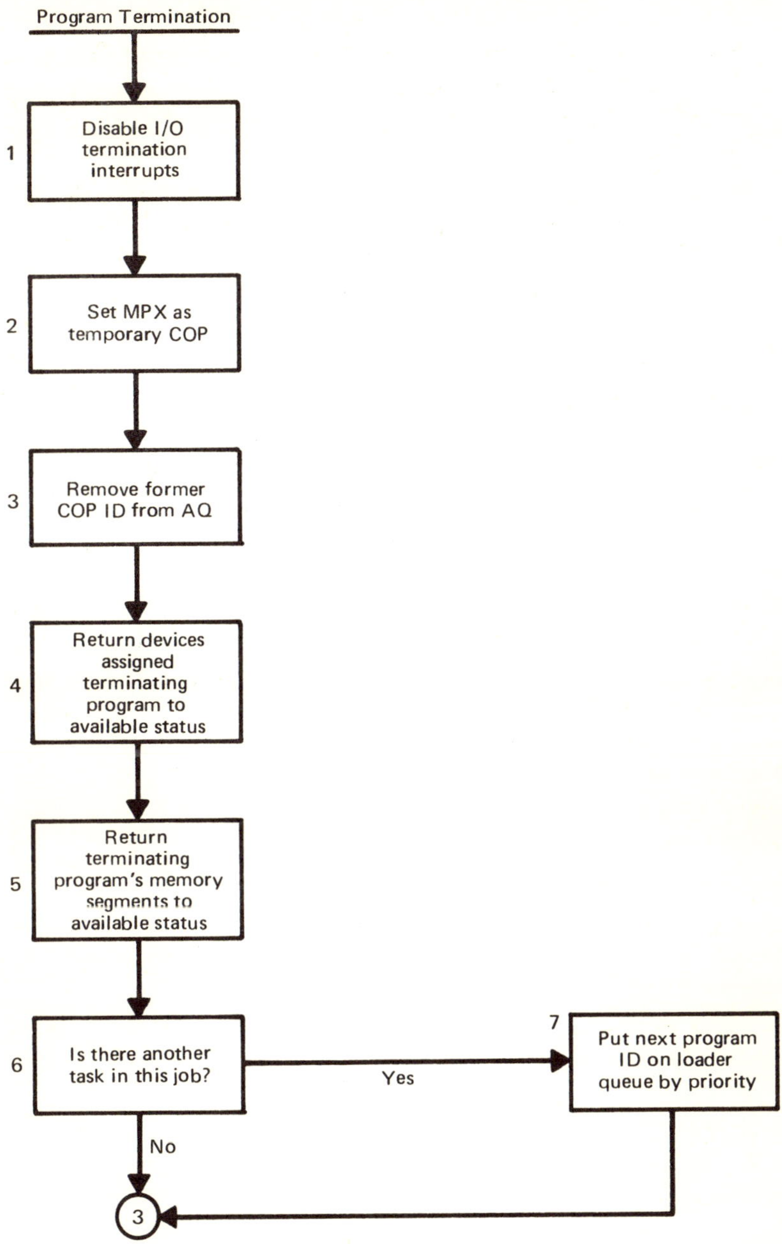

Fig. 6. Multiprogramming Executive, Flow Chart 4

grams is operated unbuffered with respect to those programs. It is this assumption that provides the three mutually exclusive states that exhaust all possibilities for a worker program, and thereby project the logic necessary for the multiprogram executive.

In the presentation of the multiprogram executive for the unbuffered case, we have used the "program ID" as the representation of the program to the executive. That is, the executive has manipulated the program ID's, in the course of which the ID's were placed into various sets each of which represents a program state. In this way then, the location of the ID within the system specifies the state of the program represented by the ID.

The program ID is an elemental, although hardly functional, form of user identification within the computing system. In the next chapter, the identification of the user is expanded and made more complete, and the ID is replaced by the "transaction." We will then be in position to identify users in terms of the "executions" they create rather than merely by searching for the programs they may have caused to be loaded. This will provide us with a useful notation for sorting out and keeping straight the logical simultaneity engendered by a number of concurrent multiprogramming activities.

CHAPTER 5

THE CPU TRANSACTION

Introduction

THE EXECUTION OF a worker program serves a purpose presumably valuable to the programmer. To accomplish this, the worker program has been logically organized to manipulate data that has a specific structure. That is, the problem whose solution is represented by the worker program determines both the worker program and the data upon which that program operates. A particular programmer is concerned about which program, of several programs, the system is executing, because the problem being solved by the computer at that moment is important if for no other reason than it determines the set of data that must be made available for that execution.

In the broad sense, one might say that the data operated upon by the programs of the operating system is worker programs. That is, the prime concern of the operating system is the manipulation of worker programs, and from this point of view it is clear that the operating system is entirely independent of what, in particular, any given worker program accomplishes. Put another way, the logic of the operating system is not based on the problem being solved by a worker program, but rather on providing that worker with sufficient facilities to solve whatever problem it was designed for. The worker programs are anonymous with respect to the kinds of problems that they solve, so that the inventory control program, for example, is effectively indistinguishable from the payroll program insofar as they are known to the operating system. If one of these is to be considered more important than the other, then this is expressed in terms of a piece of information made available to the operating system and designed for precisely that purpose, namely, a program priority variable.

Transaction Items

Thus, we see that the operating system's execution is effectively independent of the nature of particular worker programs, and is dependent only on certain data about each of them. For example, in order to execute a worker program, there are clearly certain things about that program that must be abstracted in order for the operating system to be capable of performing its assigned functions. Information is required such as the location of the program in the core memory, the amount of memory space assigned to it, and peripheral equipment assignments along with the distribution of files over these equipments. In order to resume the execution of an interrupted program, it is necessary for the operating system to have available locations in which to store the next sequential instruction and the several registers that determine the current state of the execution at the time of interruption. Furthermore, it is clearly just such data that qualifies a given execution as distinct from all other executions concurrent in the system. Hence, this data is an abstract of the execution of a particular program, so that if such a program were a reentrant code, a concurrent but distinct execution of the same program would be associated with a unique and distinct data set qualifying that execution. We shall refer to such a data set as the "transaction item" for the execution.

Figure 7 is a schematic diagram of a sample transaction item, and it indicates some of the data that it might contain. The implication of this figure is that the data for the transaction item has been arranged in physically contiguous memory locations. This is obviously not a necessary requirement for transaction items, however, since the structure of the data is required to

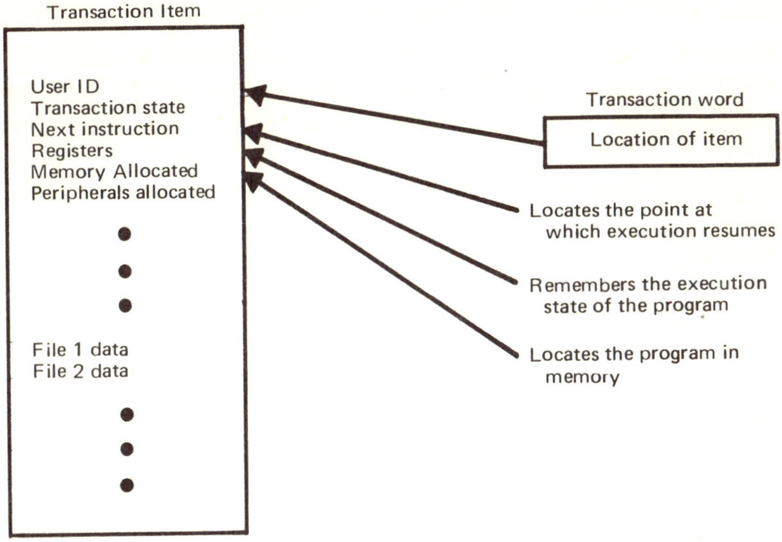

Fig. 7. Schematic Diagram of a Transaction Item

be only "logically contiguous." This means that given a starting point at which can be located a subset of a transaction item, this subset shall contain a link to the next subset of the transaction item, and so on. Hence, given a place to start, or a first location for the transaction item, the logical contiguity assures that all information in the transaction item is therefore available.

It was pointed out earlier that the operating system's function is to manipulate worker program executions. The data used to accomplish this manipulation is data about the program. This data has been abstracted from it in the form of a transaction item as described above. Therefore, the transaction item represents to the operating system everything it needs to know with regard to a given worker program. As a consequence, the transaction item represents the worker program, and, except for the physical inconvenience, could be manipulated by the operating system as the program "ID." To overcome this physical inconvenience, we associate each transaction item with a unique name.

Transaction Words

As pointed out above, the logical contiguity of the transaction item requires that it has a first or starting location. If transaction items are in the core memory, obviously the first location of a particular transaction item must indeed be unique among all transaction items. Therefore, we may take the first location for a transaction item as its name, or "ID." This will be referred to as the "transaction word."

The transaction word is a single piece of information that is convenient for manipulations by the operating system. It has no permanent location within the core memory but rather is stored in various locations according to the determinations of the operating system. The single piece of information that this transaction word carries is the core memory address of its associated transaction item. This is, of course, the first, or starting address for the transaction item from which all information contained in the transaction item may be subsequently located. Therefore, the transaction word represents the transaction item to the operating system. Since the transaction item is a unique abstract of a particular execution for a given user, it therefore follows that the transaction word is the representative to the operating system of this user and his execution of programs in the computing system.

The CPU Transaction

The computer program is a sequence of instructions. The execution of that program requires the assignment of the CPU facility, and, in order to keep that execution distinguishable from all other concurrent executions in the system, it is necessary to associate the execution with a transaction item and a transaction word. In this view then, one may think of the CPU as being "passed over" the various instructions of the program and taking the amount of time required by each of the instructions to complete its "passage." Since this execution of the program, or passage over it by the CPU, is associated directly with a transaction item and transaction word representing the particular execution, we shall say that the transaction (transaction item and transaction word) is "passed over" or "executes" this program. Because this transaction is associated directly with the execution of instructions and with the assignment of the CPU facility of the computing system for that purpose, we shall refer to it as a "CPU transaction." Thus, the CPU transaction represents the actual or imminent use of the CPU facility and serves simultaneously to identify the specific execution with which it is associated.

The CPU transacton is used to represent application of the CPU facility of the system and will serve our purposes through Chapter 7. However, in order to provide a representation for the simultaneous application of I/O facilities by a given execution, it will be necessary to determine a derivative form of the CPU transaction to be known as the "I/O transaction." This second type of a transaction is the subject of Chapter 8.

The CPU Item

When a specific transaction is associated with the CPU, it will be referred to as the "current operating transaction." We require an operating system representation for this transaction's use of the CPU while it is the current operating transaction. This will be storage locations in the core memory to be known as the "CPU item," and will consist of two fields of sufficient length to accommodate a core memory address. It is constructed as shown in Fig. 8.

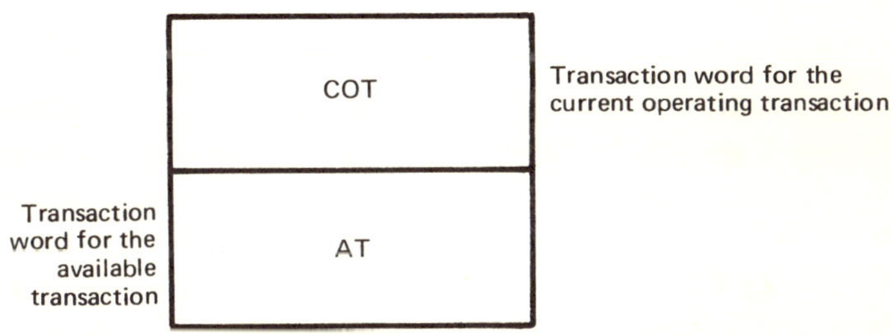

Fig. 8. Diagram of a CPU Item

The first of the two fields will contain the transaction word for the current operating transaction. Thus, the "name" of the program currently utilizing the CPU is recorded in this place in the operating system. As long as the computer is operating, it is necessary that there be some transaction word present in this field of the CPU item. When a worker program is executing, the transaction word for that worker is recorded in the CPU item, and when the operating system is executing (or some specifically designated portion of the operating system, that is, a portion represented by its own transaction), that particular transaction word is recorded here, and it represents the use of the CPU by the operating system. We refer to this field of the CPU item as the "current operating transaction field," or COT.

The second field of the CPU item is used to carry the transaction word for some transaction of current interest. This field may be either empty or contain some specific transaction that is available for manipulation by the program whose execution is represented by the current operating transaction, or COT, the transaction word for which is contained in the first field of the CPU item. We refer to this second transaction field as the "available transaction field," or AT.

The purpose of the CPU item is to represent the assignment of the CPU facility to a specific execution, and that assignment is effected, literally, by placing the transaction word for the current operating transaction into the first, or COT, field of the CPU item. Certain transactions, e.g. the operating system transaction, will execute instructions whose purpose is to manipulate other transactions (generally representing worker programs). The AT field of the CPU item is to be used as a software "register" to aid in such manipulations.

In order to strengthen the notion of the CPU item, which is an essential element in our development of a homogenous approach to the operating system, Fig. 9 gives an explicit example of a CPU item and its connection, through entries in the COT and AT fields, to transaction items in the core memory. In Fig. 9, *A* the "name" of the current operating transaction is 3000. This is the name entered into the COT field of the CPU item. Note that the COT field then points at location 3000 in the memory, which is the beginning of the collection of fields for the specific transaction item, shown in the example as transaction item 1. This transaction, and hence its associated user, have been given the symbolic name *W*1, as indicated.

The second part of this example, Fig. 9, *B*, shows that the current operating transaction is now the transaction whose "name" is 3040. This is the address of transaction item 3 in the figure whose symbolic name is *Z*. In addition, the transaction 3000, *W*1, which was formally the COT, has now become the available transaction, and therefore appears in the second field of

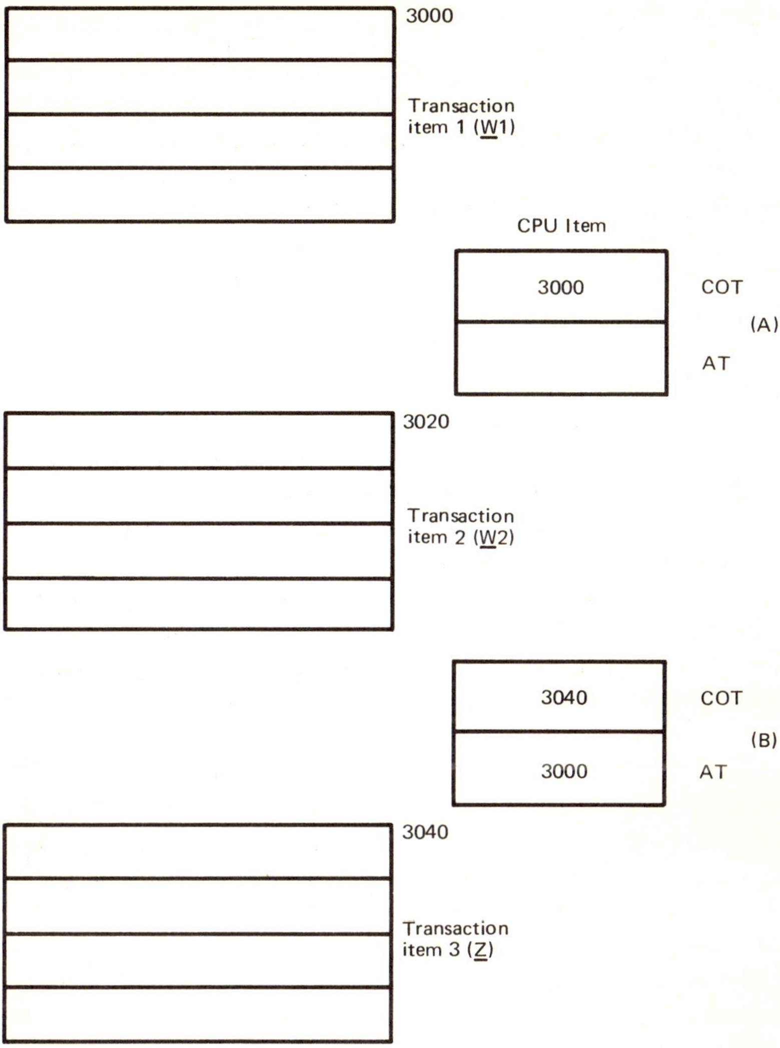

Fig. 9. Transaction Items in Core

the CPU item. Thus, the CPU item in Fig. 9, *B* shows that transaction *Z* is the current operating transaction, and transaction *W*1 is the available transaction. This, therefore, relates the assignment of the CPU to the program represented by the transaction *Z* and designates that a transaction of current interest to *Z* is the available transaction *W*1.

The O/S Function

Thus far we have associated the execution of a program with a transaction that represents that execution. The transaction is the union of the transaction item, containing all information of interest to the control of a program's execution by the operating system, and the transaction word, which is a name for the program and transaction item, and which is convenient for manipulation. We think of the transaction accomplishing the objective of the program by executing, or "passing through" it. In this way, we may say that certain logical functions are completed by a transaction by virtue of that transaction passing through the logical function.

We now consider such a logical function one that is basic to our approach to the operating system. This function is designated as the "O/S" function, and will be referred to as an entry boundary to the operating system. Its purpose is to distinguish between use of the system's facilities by programs within and without the operating system. Thus, the execution of a worker program is accomplished outside of the entry boundary of the operating system, and the execution of the operating system itself is accomplished within the boundary. In order to get to the execution of the operating system from the execution of a worker program, it is necessary to cross the O/S boundary. This crossing is accomplished by the worker transaction operating as the COT. The logical operation of the O/S function is to make the current operating transaction (for a worker program) the available transaction (AT) and to establish a specified operating system transaction as the COT.

Figure 10, *A* shows the effect of passing across an entry boundary of the operating system in schematic form. In this figure, the lines of control (the entry and exit arrows) represent the path along which the current operating transaction (no matter which one is COT) moves as it passes through the instructions being executed. In Fig. 10, *A*, the CPU item is shown before and after passing through the O/S function and the instructions that are used to implement it. Prior to entry to the O/S function, the CPU item shows that the current operating transaction is the worker transaction whose name is 3000. This has

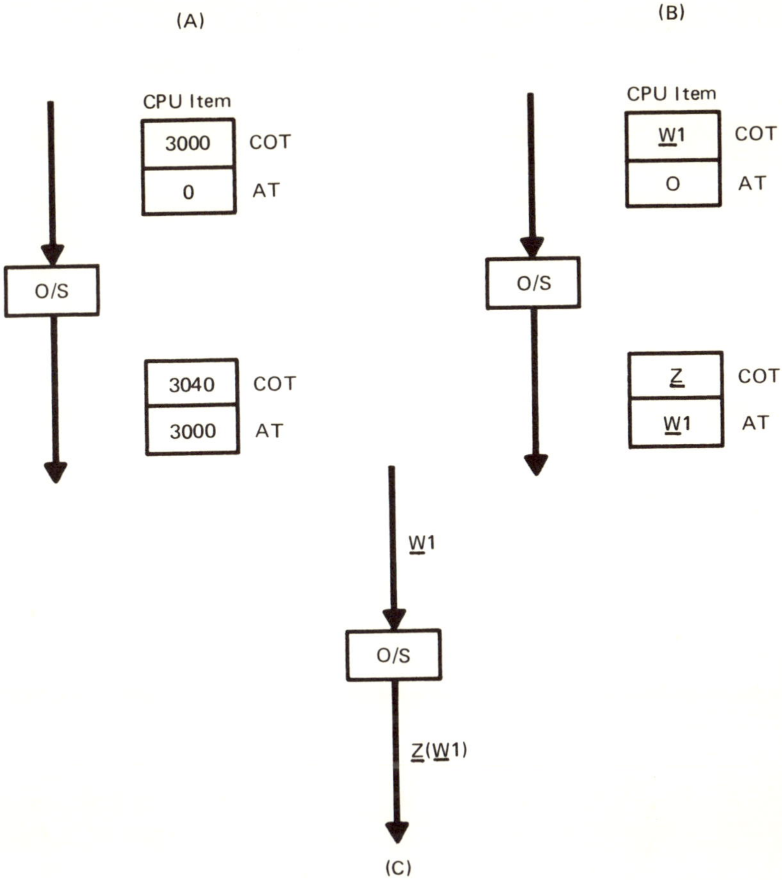

Fig. 10. Crossing an Entry Boundary of the OS

arrived from some previous function, thereby crossing the entry boundary of the operating system.

Once the execution of the O/S function has been completed, the state of the CPU item is as shown in Fig. 10, *A*, where the worker transaction 3000 has now become the available transaction, and a specific transaction, 3040, has become the COT. It is assumed that the transaction item at location 3040 in the core memory is associated with the execution of the operating system program. Thus, the operating system entry boundary has been crossed, the worker program transaction that initiated the crossing has become the available transaction, and the operating system transaction, 3040, has been established as the COT. It is this latter transaction that will now pass through the operating system program, manipulating the available transaction and any others as its logic dictates in order to carry out the required operating system functions.

The situation represented by Fig. 10, *B* is identical to that of Fig. 10, *A* described above. We have, however, substituted the symbol *W*1 for the worker transaction and the symbol *Z* for the operating system transaction. Thus, as Fig. 10, *B* indicates, prior to entry to the O/S function, *W*1 is the current operating transaction, and represents the worker program about to cross the entry boundary of the operating system. After this boundary has been crossed, the logic of the operation of the O/S function has caused *W*1 to become the available transaction, as indicated by its presence in the AT field of the CPU item, and has made the operating system transaction, *Z*, the current operating transaction by placing it in the COT field of the CPU item.

Figure 10, *C* is again the same situation discussed above, but it has a convenient notation that is more readily applicable to the transaction chart techniques to be introduced below. In this figure, the current operating transaction is the worker transaction *W*1. This is indicated by associating it with the control arrow entering the O/S function. On exit from the O/S function, the current operating transaction is *Z*, indicated as shown next to the control arrow leaving the function. Since the logic of the O/S function is to establish the current operating transaction as the available transaction after the boundary has been crossed, we so indicate this new relative position of *W*1 by enclosing it in parentheses as shown. The general form *A*(*B*), where *A* and *B* respectively stand for the COT and AT transactions, will be referred to as the "transaction term."

The Return Function

Where the O/S function represents an entry boundary to the operating system, the RETURN function serves as its exit boundary. Since the program being executed prior to the crossing of an exit boundary is the operating system, the function of the RETURN is to remove the operating system transaction, *Z*, from the COT field of the CPU item and to replace it with the transaction word of the selected execution that is to be the next COT. The transaction that replaces the operating system transaction as the COT is that one whose transaction word is contained in the AT field of the CPU item upon crossing the exit boundary.

These operations are illustrated in the schematic diagram of Fig. 11, *A*. Upon entering the RETURN function, the CPU item has the transaction word 3040 in the COT field. This is the name of the operating system transaction. In the course of its

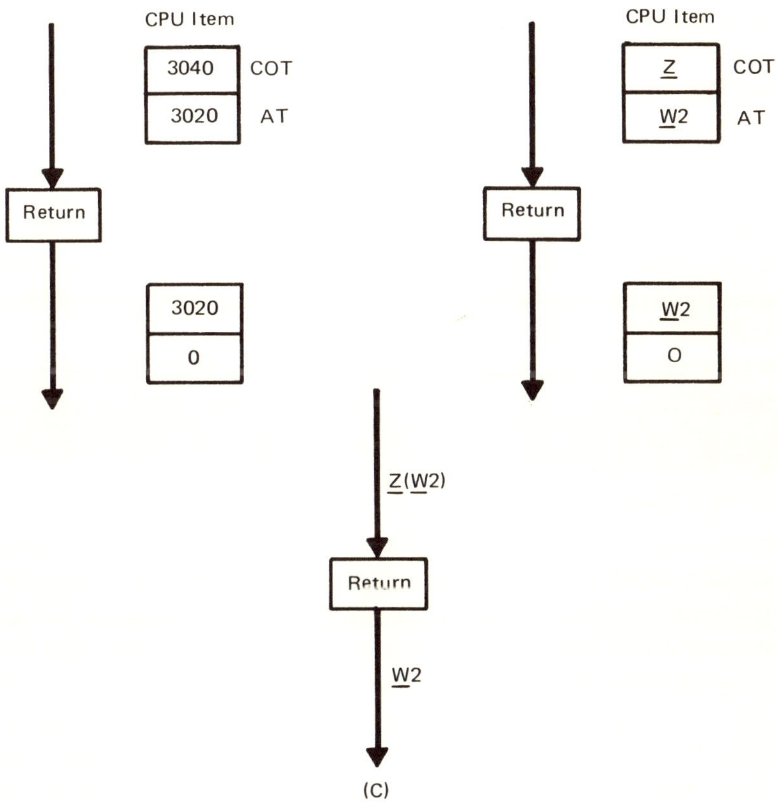

Fig. 11. Crossing an Exit Boundary of the OS

execution, the operating system has selected the (worker) transaction 3020 for installation as the next current operating transaction. It therefore appears in the AT field of the CPU item. After the RETURN function has been executed, the operating system transaction 3040 has been replaced by the selected transaction 3020 taken from the AT field. Furthermore, the AT field has been zeroed as indicated.

Figure 11, *B* is a symbolic rendition of the above described situation. Upon entering the RETURN function, the COT and AT fields of the CPU item contain the operating system transaction *Z* and the selected transaction *W*2, respectively. After the exit boundary has been crossed, the operating system transaction has been replaced by *W*2 in the COT field, and the AT field has been reset to zero.

Fig. 11, *C* is a schematic diagram showing the way in which the RETURN function will appear in our transaction charts. Here the current operating transaction *Z*, with the available transaction *W*2, is shown at the entrance to the RETURN function in the symbolic format established above for representing the COT and AT fields, respectively, of the CPU item. Upon exit from the function, our notation shows that the available transaction *W*2 has replaced the operating system transaction as the COT.

The Transaction Chart

The "transaction chart" and the more usual process or flow chart are largely identical. The major difference stems from the fact that the transaction chart, in addition to showing the actions carried out and the lines of logical control possible during the execution, features the current operating transaction and the available transaction. Furthermore, as we will see below in our transaction charts for MPX, the logical operations of major interest are those operations that effect transaction manipulation. Thus, the actual technique for determining whether or not a specific I/O is ready for initiating the input/output operation is of little interest in a transaction chart; we are only interested in the point of its occurrence and the effect on the transactions of the CPU term.

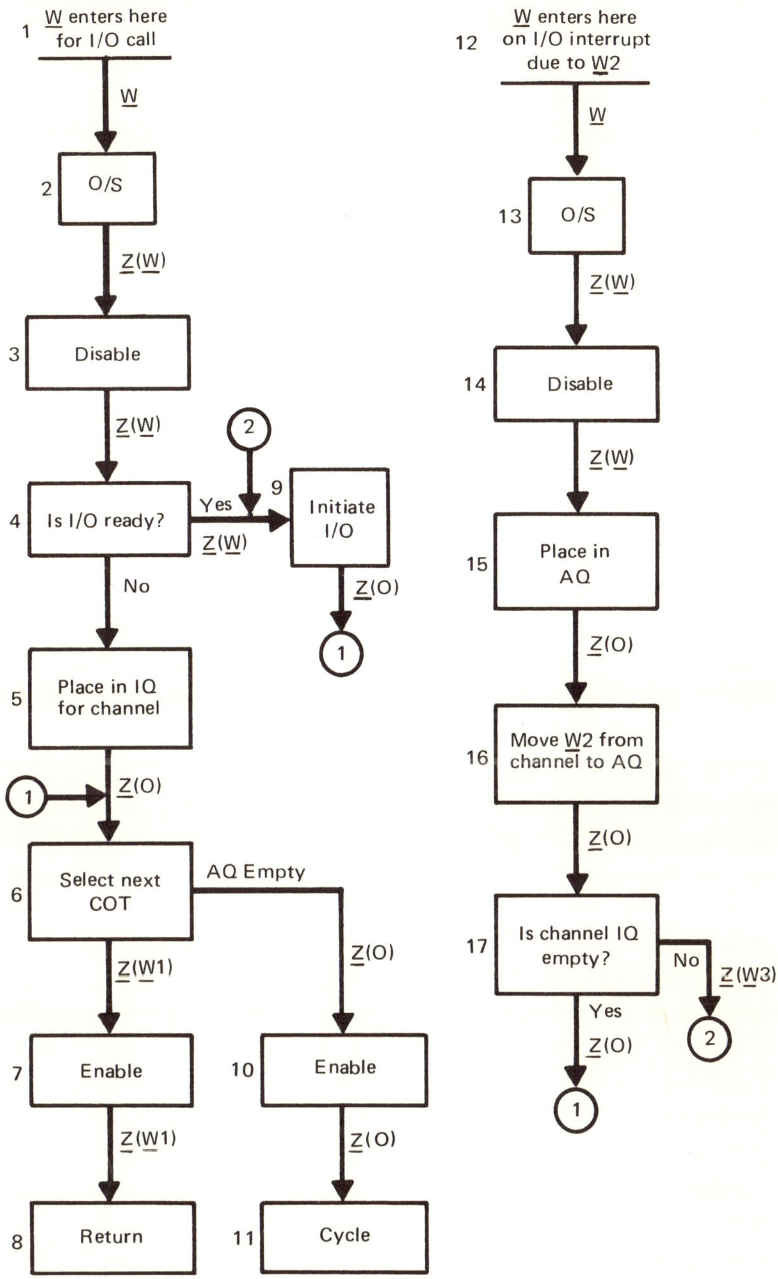

Fig. 12. MPX Transaction Chart

Transaction Chart for MPX

Figure 12 is a transaction chart showing the operations carried out by the MPX for unbuffered executions, described in Chapter 4, upon entry by a worker program as the current operating transaction, or due to an interrupt that stems from an I/O termination.

The entry for an I/O call by a worker program is made in box 1. We represent the "name" of this program, i.e. its transaction word, by the generic symbol *W***.** Since *W* is the COT on this entrance, we indicate this by writing the symbol for this worker program next to the control arrow leading from box 1. Thus, the current operating transaction that crosses the operating system boundary by execution of the O/S function at box 2 is *W*. The transaction which is COT upon exit from box 2, however, is the operating system transaction *Z*, and *W* has become the available transaction, as indicated.

The transaction *Z*, as the current operating transaction, now passes through MPX, and its first function is to disable all further I/O interrupts. This does not alter the state of the CPU item so that on exit from box 3 the current operating transaction is still *Z* and *W* remains as the available transaction.

The function of box 4 is to ascertain whether or not the I/O operation required by the available transaction *W* can be carried out at this time. The proper execution of such a function depends on the particular I/O requirement and hardware configuration of the system in which the MPX is being executed. Thus, for example, I/O READY may require that the channel, controller, and device be available in one system, whereas in a second system using a multiplexor it might only be necessary that the device be available for the I/O to be ready. Whichever is the case, the important point here is that the question is asked, and furthermore, that the question is asked relative to the available transaction carried in the AT field of the CPU item.

However the I/O READY function is to be executed, the data necessary for its execution, relative to the transaction word carried in the AT field, will be found in the transaction item pointed to by that transaction word. Thus in a programming context, we may say that *Z* executes the I/O READY subroutine, with W as the single item in the calling sequence. In this interpretation then, W is akin to an indirect address for the true calling sequence.

Whichever of the two alternatives offered by the I/O READY function is chosen, there is no transformation effected on the CPU term $Z(W)$. We shall, however, assume for the moment that the I/O operation for W is ready, thereby causing the function in box 9 to be executed.

The state of the CPU item is expressed by the CPU term on entering box 9. This is identical to that term which entered box 4, so that as before, in the case of the I/O READY function, the INITIATE I/O function shown in box 9 will operate on the contents of the AT field of the CPU item, treating it as an indirect reference to an actual calling sequence. Thus, the function of box 9 refers to the data in the transaction item W, which is pertinent to the required I/O operation. Again, the detailed execution of the INITIATE I/O function is dependent on the particular equipment. What is important for the purposes of a transaction chart is the transformation of the input CPU term that box 9 accepts. In particular, as we described in Chapter 4, the initiation of an unbuffered I/O for a particular worker program must be accompanied by actions that place the ID for the program into the proper word of a reference list that associates this ID with an I/O termination. In the present context, the ID is the transaction word. Therefore, an additional function of box 9 is to remove the transaction word from the AT field of the CPU item and to place that transaction word into the proper position in the reference list. The AT field is then reset to zero and the actual I/O initiated, after which the required operations for the INITIATE I/O function have been completed.

Since the available transaction, W, has been removed from the AT field of the CPU item, the CPU term that exits from box 9 is altered. The alteration in this case is in the AT field of the CPU item with the transaction W no longer appearing as the quantity in parentheses in the CPU term. The COT is still the transaction Z, i.e. the operating system, and the line of control indicates that there is a transfer to connector 1.

We now return to box 4 and the I/O READY function, assuming that for the transaction *W* in the entering CPU term to this box, the I/O was not ready. There is no transformation in the term, and therefore *W* remains the available transaction for manipulation by the current operating transaction, *Z*, upon entrance to box 5. Since the I/O required by *W* is not possible for initiation at this time, unbuffered execution requires that further execution of the worker program represented by *W* be deferred until the required I/O operation can be initiated. As described in Chapter 4 in our discussion of MPX, a transaction awaiting access to a particular channel is placed in an initiation queue for that channel, from which it is removed in turn when the channel becomes available. This then is the meaning of the function shown in box 5. The entering CPU term is transformed by box 5 to the extent that the available transaction carried in the AT field of the CPU item is removed and placed, according to the established priority rule, into the proper initiation queue. The AT field is then reset to zero, so that now the CPU term on exit shows that there is no available transaction.

The exit from box 5 leads through connector 1 to box 6. Furthermore, the entry to box 6 requires that *Z* be the current operating transaction and that the AT field of the CPU item be reset to zero. This requirement is met by the CPU term on exit from box 9. Since this is the only condition on the entering CPU term that is satisfactory for entrance to box 6, all entrances to this box, from whatever portion of the operating system, must meet this CPU term condition.

The purpose of box 6 is to cause the selection of a transaction from those residing in the AQ, i.e. the programs available for execution, and to place the selected transaction into the AT field of the CPU item. Thus, we enter box 6 with the CPU term *Z*(O) and exit box 6 with the transaction word of the selected transaction in the AT field. The CPU term on exit from box 6 is as shown in the figure, where the selected transaction is represented by the symbol *W*1.

With the next COT in the AT field of the CPU item, the transaction *Z* now passes through box 7 where the interrupts are enabled, and then through box 8 to execute the RETURN function. This crosses the exit boundary of the operating system, thereby establishing *W* as the COT, and resuming the execution of the program associated with this transaction word.

Returning now to box 6, where the selection of the next COT is made, let us suppose that the AQ is empty. This can occur only because all worker transactions in the system are either seeking to initiate I/O operations and are waiting in initiation queues, or are awaiting the termination of I/O operations that have already been initiated. In all events, if the AQ is determined to be empty during execution of MPX due to an I/O call by a transaction; then it is known that there is at least one transaction in the system that will ultimately be returned to the AQ. Hence, it is necessary for the transaction *Z*, representing the operating system, to enable the I/O termination interrupts (box 10) and at box 11 to begin cycling, there to await the arrival of a termination interrupt whose processing will bring a transaction word into the AQ. Note that boxes 10 and 11 are entered with the AT field of the CPU item remaining zero, since selection of a COT was not possible.

We consider now the sequence of operations when an I/O interrupt occurs. Let us suppose that this interrupt is due to the I/O operation generated to satisfy the requirements of a transaction *W*2. The transaction effected by this interrupt is the COT, and for this discussion we give it the symbolic name *W*. Thus, at box 12 we enter the interrupt processing portion of MPX with *W* as the COT. The interrupting transaction is *W*2, as mentioned earlier. Crossing the entry boundary of the operating system at box 13 makes *Z* the current operating transaction and places *W*, the interrupted transaction, into the AT field of the CPU item. At box 14 further termination interrupts are disabled, and at box 15 the available transaction (*W*) is placed into the availability queue since this transaction is still in state 3 (available for execution). On exit from box 15, the AT field of the CPU item has been reset to zero. The function of box 16 is to determine from the interrupt data available, the location of the reference list word corresponding to the interrupt. The transaction word *W*2, for which the I/O has terminated, is retrieved from this reference list word and is moved to the availability queue, since it represents an execution whose I/O is now complete and which may now go into state 3. This does not effect the CPU term *Z*(O), as shown on exit from box 16.

The function of box 17 is to determine if there are any transactions in the intiation queue for the channel associated with the present termination interrupt. If the associated initiation queue is empty, then there is no opportunity at this time to initiate an I/O operation on this channel, and no transaction word is picked up as an available transaction by the COT. The next step is to transfer to connector 1 with the CPU term as shown, noting that it satisfies the entry requirements to box 6.

On the other hand, if there is a transaction word awaiting

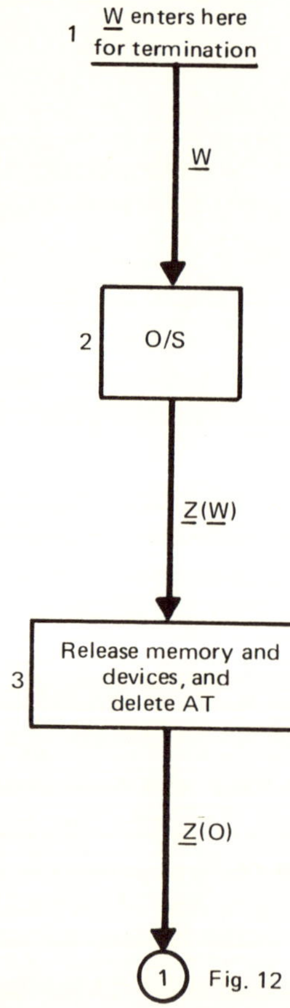

Fig. 13. Program Termination

access to the channel that has just terminated its I/O activity, then that transaction word is picked up as the available transaction, and appears in the AT field of the CPU item. Thus, the CPU term on this exit from box 17 is $Z(W3)$, where $W3$ is the transaction retrieved from the associated initiation queue. The tranfer indicated takes us to the entrance to box 9, where again it should be noted that the CPU term required for entry to this box is correct. Here then, the I/O operation for $W3$ is initiated, the transaction word $W3$ is moved from the AT field to the reference list word associated with the channel, and the AT field is reset to zero as indicated. This is followed by the transfer to box 1, where the next COT is selected by the operating system transaction Z.

We complete our description of MPX in terms of its transaction chart by considering the program termination entrance. The chart for these operations is shown in Fig. 13.

The worker program that is terminating is associated with the transaction W. Upon termination, the worker program transfers to MPX, and therefore it is the worker program itself, acting as COT, that crosses the entry boundary to the operating system at this point. This establishes the operating system transaction Z as the COT, and places the worker transaction W into the AT field of the CPU item. Next, at box 3, using the transaction word as the pointer to its transaction item, the memory and devices allocated to the available transaction W are returned to MPX, and the transaction word in the AT field is discarded. Note that on exit from box 3, the COT is the operating system transaction Z, and the AT field has been reset to zero so that there is no available transaction. Therefore, control is transferred to connector 1 of Fig. 12 where a selection of the next COT is made from the availability queue. Again it should be noted that the CPU term Z(O) is correct for entry to box 6.

Summary Remark

By repeating our analysis of the MPX for unbuffered executions in transaction terms, we have achieved an objective that will have wide elaboration and application throughout the remainder of this book. The concept of the CPU item with its COT and AT fields and the resultant symbolic transaction terminology will be used as the basic tool for describing and analyzing the operating system structures to be introduced subsequently. In fact, the power of transaction analysis becomes evident when we apply these techniques to the specification of the so-called "acceptance" and "presentation" portions of an operating system. For it is with this method that we are able to represent the independent, asynchronous operation of the various functional modules of multiprogramming systems in a unifying and meaningful way that exposes the dynamic topology they contain.

CHAPTER 6

THE BASIC FUNCTIONS

Introduction

IN CHAPTER 4, we examined the structure of a multiprogram executive as it is derived from the assumption of unbuffered input-output activity on the part of the worker program. In Chapter 5, we introduced the CPU transaction and then expressed the structure of the unbuffered I/O demand executive of Chapter 4 in terms of a transaction analysis. It is stressed however, that in each of these chapters only the executive of the operating system was under consideration, and that up to this point nothing has been said concerning other aspects of the operating system outside of the executive.

The multiprogram executive, whether for buffered or unbuffered I/O demand multiprogramming, must necessarily occupy the dominant position in the logical hierarchy of all operating system functions. This is due to the fact that the execution of the executive is accomplished for the purpose of allocating the CPU and I/O equipments of the system to the various transactions of the multiprogram set seeking access to it. In the relatively simple case of MPX for unbuffered I/O demand multiprogramming, the allocation of the CPU and I/O equipments and the handling of the I/O terminations cause the several transactions of the multiprogrammed set to be moved among the three possible states. These changes of state involve the handling of queues on the part of MPX and, therefore, it is clear that the execution of the executive must be accomplished without intervention due to interrupts. It is for this reason that MPX occupies the prime position in the operating system.

In the present chapter, we initiate consideration of the remainder of the operating system, examining those functions that may be thought of as the environment of the multiprogram executive. The discussions in the pages that follow identify both basic functions that must be a part of every operating system and some of the structural arrangements between those functions. Of fundamental importance, however, is the fact that the general qualities ascribed to these functions do not depend on whether the MPX used is for buffered or unbuffered I/O demand multiprogramming.

Computer System Facilities

The computer systems that we shall consider will have a single CPU, a specified amount of core memory, a number of peripheral devices of various types, and the necessary data channels to link devices and memory. Consider now an application program that is executed by such a system. In the first place, it is presented to the computer in the form of a "job" that appears on a suitable media at one of the computer's entry devices, e.g. the card reader. Secondly, the job describes, usually in large scale terms, the "steps" to be taken in accomplishing the job, and perhaps something about the distribution of files to devices, core memory requirements, overall running time, and a remark or two concerning printed or punched output. In the third place, the job also contains, or designates, the program, or programs, to be executed in order to accomplish the job.

Our point of view will be that the various hard facilities of the computer, the CPU, the core memory, and so on, and the several "soft" facilities that are for the present loosely referred to as the operating system must be made available to the job in order to complete its execution. To put this another way, an operating system facility is required in order to recognize the presence of a job at the job entry device. A second operating system facility is required to interpret the job description and then to provide the worker programs of the job with both the CPU facility and the required portion of the core memory facility. During the use of the CPU facility (and implicitly, the allocated core memory facility) by the instructions of the application program, demands for the use of input-output facilities will arise. Clearly, these facilities must be made available if the job is to complete, and in so doing will often require the temporary assignment of certain soft facilities of the operating system, such as the I/O package. More importantly, a job must be supplied with all facilities that it requires as its execution generates those requirements. We shall consider it to be the function, and indeed the purpose of the operating system to satisfy all such requirements.

General Discussion

In a multiprogramming system, the CPU facility of the computer is distributed over a number of concurrently present worker programs. More directly, concurrent worker programs in a multiaccess environment have programs resident in a common core memory, from which point they sequentially share access to the computer's CPU and the various peripheral devices associated with the system. Hence, multiprogramming may be thought of as the concurrent execution of a set of programs that are simultaneously resident within the system. We have referred earlier to such a set of programs as the multiprogram set.

It is clear that in order to add a program to the multiprogram set, certain programs will be required to carry out the necessary functions in an orderly fashion. More particularly, it is necessary to introduce the user's job request data into the computer system, i.e. to read it from the external media into the computer's memory so that the next actions may be taken. Thus, although job request data may exist externally to the computer environment, nothing can be done with it until it has been brought into the environment for further action. This is a basic function of any operating system, and it is at this point that we say that the processing of a job request begins.

Once this job request data has been brought into the computer and is available for further processing, a function is necessary to interpret the job request and to determine how the system can best meet the user's requirement. This is a second basic function.

The efforts of a computer system on behalf of its users is limited to whatever can be accomplished by the execution of a computer program. Hence, the interpretation of a job request must necessarily result in identification of programs to be executed. However, before such execution can be carried out these programs must be loaded into the computer system memory, so that operation of a loader program is a third basic function of an operating system.

Once the programs necessary for satisfying the job request have been brought into the memory, they are considered as being in the multiprogram set and from this point seek access to the various facilities of the computer system. At any given moment there may be a number of programs seeking access to, say, the CPU facility of the system, and therefore there must be some function within the operating system that determines which of the several programs seeking use of this facility is to be given access to it. Similarly, if there are several programs in the multiprogram set seeking access to a common peripheral device, such as a random access disk, for which there is a single information channel between core memory and device, then some portion of the operating system must likewise determine which of these programs is next to be allowed to carry out its data transfer operation. The portion of the operating system charged with responsibility for determining order of access among the worker routines of a multiprogram set is the multiprogram executive.

As worker programs are given access to the CPU and peripheral device facilities of the computer system, their execution may lead them to preparation of data for output to a particular "presentation device" associated with the system. Examples of such devices are the card punch, paper tape punch, and printer. In general, a presentation device is a peripheral device that can be used sensibly only by a single program at a time. Such devices also usually have the property of being relatively slow. Data to be delivered to a presentation device is referred to as "presentation data."

In a multiprogramming environment, difficulties arise because there may be a number of worker programs in the mutiprogram set that are producing output concurrently for a common presentation device. Hence, there must be some mechanism for controlling this output, and the approach to be considered will employ two functions. The first function accepts presentation data from a worker program and organizes it with previous presentation data from this routine on a mass storage unit. The second function retrieves presentation data from this storage unit and directs it to the proper presentation device. It should be clear, however, that this second function must seize the presentation device required by the worker program for the duration of its presentation data production. It is therefore incumbent on this function that it maximize the presentation data production rate on the selected presentation device.

In the following sections of this chapter, we discuss each of these several operating system functions in greater detail and then certain generalities concerning their dynamic interrelationships.

The Receiver

Whenever the operating system has been notified (by whatever means are available in the particular system) that there exists job request data on a particular external device, it is necessary to execute a function that inputs this job request data and carries out several associated operations. This function will be called the receiver, and when executed brings the job request data into the computer system memory and carries out any necessary validation and message assembly operations that are required. It then establishes a call for the execution of the next function of the operating system that is required in order to treat this just received job request data.

A job request may be thought of as a string of characters, including punctuation, that has been separated by the nature of its media (e.g., cards) into fixed size units. In many systems therefore, one practical requirement on the receiver function might be the elimination of trailing spaces in each card read, and concatenation of the input with suitable sentinel characters.

In addition, many systems will allow a number of job requests to be mounted together on the job request input device. Thus, for example, several job requests may appear in the card deck currently being read by the receiver function. In this case, it is also necessary for the receiver to recognize an "end of job request" so as to separate these job requests.

The language for expressing a job request varies extensively from system to system. In cases where the language available is quite large, it is likely that users will taken advantage of the capabilities offered so that individual job requests will tend to be large as well. As a consequence, it may therefore be necessary to store received job requests on an external storage media, such as a disk or drum. This requires of the receiver function not only that it prepare the incoming job requests in a format suited to storage on the particular device, but also that it pass the location of this job request on the device into the operating system along with the identification for the job.

It should be evident from the above discussion that if the job request is passed by the receiver function from the job request input device through the core memory and out again to some external storage medium, then some explicit form of job identification is required at this stage of the job's progress through the system. Further, this identification must be in the core memory, or otherwise the remainder of the operating system will have no means for being aware of the presence of this job. The obvious mechanism is, of course, the CPU transaction, consisting of transaction item and identifying transaction word as defined in Chapter 5. It may therefore be an additional function of the receiver to find core memory space for a transaction item to be associated with the new job request. The transaction item then provides the ideal location for storing any data pertaining to the newly received job request such as, for example, the location of the job request on the storage media.

In many computing systems, the job request language itself is somewhat restricted, and in particular the length of a job request may be restricted. Certain on-line query systems have this property in their query languages. Thus, for example, if we think of each query addressed to an on-line reservation system as a job request, the language of this job request will generally be very highly structured and limited in the number of allowable characters. In such circumstances then, the necessity for passing the job request to an external storage media may not arise. Again, the transaction item may be considered as the ideal core memory location in which to store such a job request.

The Director

A job request is a string of characters in a format and with a structure that should be easily readable by the user. This language is obviously not suited to the needs of the computer, and therefore must be translated into a suitable set of codes from which its meaning may be interpreted. The function carrying the responsibility for these operations will be referred to as the director. In addition, the director may include a scheduling function by means of which it ascertains which of a collection of jobs seeking access to the computer system are to be next activated by being allowed access to the loader function described below. Thus, the director may schedule the work load for the computer system. Finally, the director may be the point at which peripheral devices and/or memory are allocated to programs, although we shall generally assume that such functions are the responsibility of the loader.

A typical approach to the inclusion of the director function in an operating system is to combine the director with the receiver. The job request is read, the individual elements of the request language are interpreted, and the result is then passed to an external storage device for later examination by the loader function. As mentioned above for the receiver, it would be necessary for the director to record the location of this interpreted data on the peripheral device. This location would then have to appear in the core memory, for which purpose the transaction item associated with the job would serve well.

If the job control language is extensive, then the program implementing the director function will in all likelihood be extremely large. In this case, consideration might be given to loading the director programs as required for the servicing of a batch of job requests, rather than keeping the director function permanently resident in the core memory. This assumes, of course, that the time required for job executions is large relative to the frequency of job requests and the consequent requirement for execution of the director function. If, on the other hand, there is a high frequency of job requests resulting in jobs whose execution is relatively short, the cost to continually reload the programs that implement the director function may be excessive.

As mentioned above, the allocation of peripheral devices and core memory to the new jobs may be assigned as a subfunction of the director. It should be noted, however, that both of these activities should be carried out in the director, rather than one of them by this function, and the other in the loader or other independent and possibly asynchronous subfunction. The reason for this is that if, for example, peripheral device allocation is carried out in the director and is successfully accomplished for a given job, while at a later time in a separate function core memory allocation for the job is attempted but fails, then the delay of this job for lack of core memory space unnecessarily ties up the assigned peripheral devices, making them unavailable to other jobs which then may be improperly delayed. In view of this, one possibility for peripheral device and core memory allocation for newly received jobs is to accomplish it as a subsidiary function of the director. This makes the loading of the programs for such jobs an urgent and even mandatory requirement on the remainder of the operating system. On the other hand, if these two activities are reserved to the loader function, last minute determinations based on the sequence in which currently executing jobs are terminating allow the loader to make more effective choices of the order in which new jobs are to be allocated and their executions initiated.

The Loader

Job request data that has been brought into the computer via the receiver and interpreted by the director, is now represented in terms of a request to allocate memory for, and load, certain programs. The function of the loader is to find the required programs on the peripheral device storing them, allocate memory, and, if necessary in the particular system, relocate the program into the allocated memory space.

There are three classes of peripheral devices generally sought by application programs. These are the *initial input*, *intermediate*, and *presentation* devices. Initial input devices accept media that the user brings to the computer. Such media are cards, magnetic tapes, disk packs, and so on. Thus an initial input device will provide source data on which the application program will operate. Since the user determines the nature of this initial input, the particular type of input device required by the program is determined for the operating system and must be assigned accordingly. The intermediate devices are used as external scratch output and input by the application programs. In general, the particular devices to be employed for this purpose are of secondary importance to the user, so that the selection of intermediate devices for the execution of a job may be entirely at the discretion of the loader function. The presentation devices are low speed sequential output devices, the most important example of which is the printer. In general, such devices are not assigned to the execution of a job, but rather are applied to producing the output from that job after the output has been stored on an intermediate device, such as a disk pack.

The allocation of core memory is a difficult problem which has received extensive treatment in the literature. The method employed for core memory allocation is to a large extent dependent on the method of memory addressing made available by the computer design, along with the memory protection mechanisms if that is a feature present in the computer system. In general, however, the allocation of core memory might be broken into two large categories referred to as "contiguous" and "noncontiguous" allocation.

The allocation of memory space on a contiguous basis implies that all required core memory locations are found in a physically contiguous unit. Allocation on a noncontiguous basis implies that the required core memory locations are the aggregate of *blocks* of core memory locations. These blocks are generally not physically contiguous in the core memory. It should also be pointed out that whether or not the memory space required for the instructions of the program is allocated on a contiguous or noncontiguous basis, a certain amount of contiguous allocation will generally be required for the working, or data, space associated with the program. This is due to the fact that linearly organized data sets, such as lists and arrays, input-output buffer areas, and so on, must, by the very nature of the algorithms that refer to them in applications programs, necessarily lie in contiguous memory space. This is not a mandatory requirement, however, for collections of independently named program variables.

The receiver, director, and loader are referred to generally as the "acceptance portion" of the system.

The Multiprogram Executive

The multiprogram executive determines the order of access of the programs in the multiprogram set to certain facilities of the computer system. These facilities are the CPU, the channels, and the peripheral devices. Thus the MPX function includes the so-called I/O package and the associated interrupt processing. Those computations necessary to determine which, among the competing worker programs, is next given the CPU for its execution, is also considered a part of the MPX function.

The Distributor

The distributor is the first of the two functions described earlier for transmitting presentation data from the worker program to the designated presentation device. It is the responsbility of the distributor program to accept all presentation data records prepared by worker programs in the multiprogram set and to direct these to locations in a mass storage device. The organization of blocks of records in this external storage, and their accounting, is the function of the distributor program as well. In addition, it may carry out certain standard editing functions for worker programs, operating on the presentation data records that it receives.

The Dispatcher

The dispatcher is the second function of the "presentation portion" of the system, and is closely associated with the workings of the distributor function. In general, it is the responsibility of the dispatcher to read the presentation data from designated positions in the external storage and to use this data to drive the associated presentation devices at maximum throughput rates.

The details of storage methods best suited to the joint operation of distributor and dispatcher functions is generally beyond the scope of the present work and depend largely on the specific peripheral device equipments made available. Some general statements concerning the methods to be employed can be made, however, when it is considered that there is generally a multiplicity of users seeking access to the presentation devices of the system. From our point of view, the access to presentation devices is equivalent to access to the distributor function, which channels presentation data from all sources to a common external storage. Evidently then, the peripheral device to be employed by the distributor and dispatcher functions will have to be capable of random access. Furthermore, it is necessary for the distributor to so organize all presentation data destined for a specific presentation device, e.g. the printer, from a given program into a logically sequential structure on the random access device. This is required in order that the dispatcher, when it is ready to handle the presentation data for the particular application program, can find all presentation data for that program in the proper sequence on the device. Furthermore, this organization of the logical sequence of records must be fairly efficient, so that the dispatcher program is not saddled with excessive calculations to determine the location of the next record in the random access device. Otherwise, if extensive computations must be made by the dispatcher, then not only is valuable CPU time lost to the execution of application programs, but in addition output delays to the presentation device may occur, with resultant start/stop penalties at the presentation device and consequent reduction in its throughput performance.

It is with the objective in mind of minimizing the amount of CPU time required by the dispatcher that subfunctions to be carried out by the dispatcher function are minimized. In particular, any editing or general data transformation functions that must be carried out are reserved for the distributor function.

The six basic functions necessary for a multiprogramming operating system, along with some of the subfunctions that they might carry out, are listed below.

Receiver
- job request input
- input routing
- system log
- message validation

Director
- job request interpretation
- code conversion
- formatting
- decryption
- message verification

Loader
- program loading
- memory allocation
- relocation
- linking
- reloading (for roll-in, roll-out systems)

Executive
- CPU distribution
- I/O distribution
- memory protection
- interrupt processing
- channel utilization priority
- random access device priority
- buffering control
- file reference control
- I/O rate control

Distributor
- presentation output processing
- code conversion
- formatting
- encryption
- external storage management

Dispatcher
- presentation output control
- device throughput optimization

Interrelationships

Each of the functions described above for the passage of a user job request and attendant programs through the system carries out certain operations relative to the job request data, and to the worker programs designated by the job request data, and any presentation data they generate. Generally speaking, the course of a job through the system begins with the receiver, proceeds to the director and the loader, and then as current operating transaction, executes to completion under control of the executive. In the course of the execution, presentation data is developed, and that data passes through the distributor and dispatcher to the presentation data devices.

The flow of a job through a system is expressed in rough diagrammatic form in Fig. 14. The job request, in passing through the receiver, can generate two explicit actions; the job request data is sent to storage locations, either internal or external, depending upon the design of the system, and a notification to process the job request is made available to the director. In the figure, the call for execution of the director is indicated by placing such a notification in a queue, called here DIRQ, associated with the director. Whether one or many such calls are allowed to be concurrently resident in this queue is a question of system design.

Whatever the technique, the execution of the director involves three major actions. In the first place, the job request data stored by the receiver is made available to the director and is examined by it. The consequence of this examination is loading data that is prepared in accordance with specifications for the loader, and this data is then stored in locations, either internal or external, for use by the loader function. Finally, once the loading data has been prepared and placed in its storage location, a call is established for the operation of the loader. This call is indicated in Fig. 14 as being placed in a loader queue, LDRQ.

As in the case of execution of the director, there are three major actions involved in carrying out the loader function. First, loading data is read from the assigned storage and is interpreted in terms of the programs that must be loaded from whatever

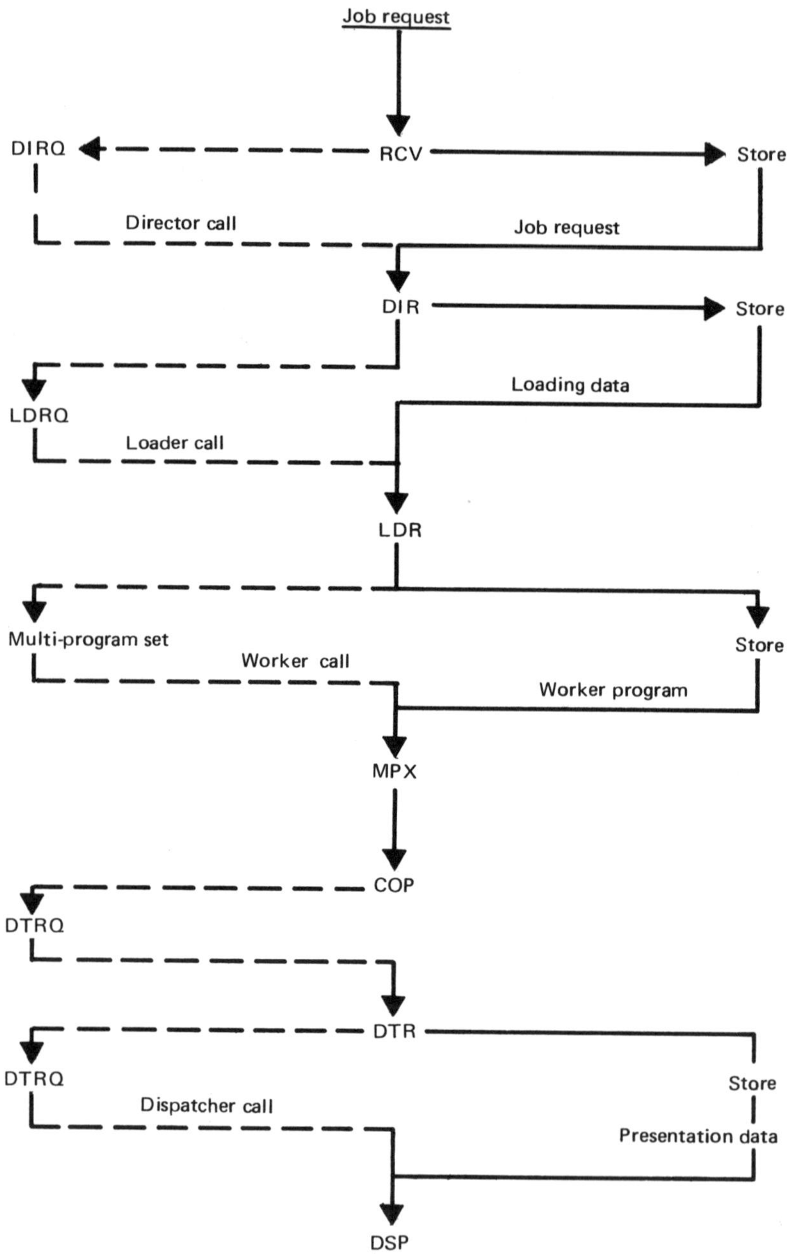

Fig. 14. Movement of the Job Through the System

peripheral medium is used to hold them. Once it has been determined what programs are to be read into the memory (and allocations for both core memory and peripheral devices have been carried out), the second major activity for the loader function is to locate these programs on their peripheral devices and to load and relocate these programs into the allocated memory space. When loading has been completed, the job request is represented by the worker program that is now resident in the memory, so that the final action of the loader is to send a notation to the executive that makes it aware of the presence of this addition to the multiprogram set.

The major function of the multiprogram executive (MPX) is to determine which of the workers in the multiprogram set is to be given access to system facilities that are sought concurrently. In particular, one of the programs will be given access to the CPU (currently being used by MPX to make its determination). When this occurs, we refer to the worker program receiving the CPU as the current operating program, or COP. In particular, at the time MPX is being executed in order to determine which of the workers in the multiprogram set is to be the next COP, the MPX itself is COP.

For the worker program that has become COP, Fig. 14 shows that it performs two major functions relative to the operating system as it executes. These are to develop presentation data, and to establish a call for the distributor to handle this presentation data. We have shown the call for distributor action as being resident on a distributor queue, DTRQ.

The major action that the distributor carries out during its execution is to accept the presentation data input from the COP and to transfer this information into specified locations on an external mass storage device. For each of the presentation devices controlled by the distributor and the dispatcher, it is necessary for the distributor to associate new presentation data output with a particular data group that is identified by the worker program producing it. This is a separate file control problem that is divorced from the concept of the distributor function in a multiprogramming operating system and, as such, is not considered further here.

The final function in a multiprogramming operating system is the dispatcher. Its purpose is to operate each of the presentation data devices in such a fashion as to maximize the throughput on the devices while at the same time preserving the order of presentation data output. Intermixing of distinct outputs from different worker programs that are destined for a common presentation device must be prevented. Hence, the major actions taken by the dispatcher function are related to the external storage and the presentation devices, reading blocks of data from the former and transferring the individual records in these blocks to the latter. The major problem facing the designer of a properly operating dispatcher is the efficient location of the next data group for output relative to the given presentation device. As in the case of the distributor, however, the explicit methods for accomplishing this are secondary in this work to the fact of its accomplishment.

Transactions

The execution of the several functions in the acceptance, executive, and presentation portions of an operating system causes the job request to be passed through the computer system. As we have discussed it in Chapter 5, the execution of the job itself is represented by a CPU transaction. Since each function of an operating system is associated with a program that is executed, we may assign transactions to them. Thus, the transactions involved with execution of the acceptance portion create a job transaction for the new job and pass that transaction into the multiprogram set. It is this job transaction on which the executive and presentation portions operate in order to complete the passage of the job through the system. In the paragraphs that follow, the basic functions of the operating system are reviewed from this transaction point of view.

The Acceptance Portion

Either by the testing of an external switch or by the generation of an internal interrupt, the operating system is notified of the presence of a job request on a peripheral input device. This is the point at which the system has its first awareness of the user, and therefore is also the moment of origin of the transaction representing that user, taking the form of a transaction item and its associated transaction word. The transaction item will initially contain information such as the identity of the user and the device on which the job request is available, and is assigned locations in the core memory. Then the transaction word (pointing at the core memory locations for the transaction item) for this job request is placed in a location (RCVQ) that makes it available to the receiver function. Thus, when the receiver is executed, examination of the transaction word leads the receiver to the transaction item for the job, and thereby provides it with the necessary information for reading in the job request data from the peripheral device.

Once the job request data has been read in by the receiver, and any necessary processing, such as validation, carried out, the job request data is moved to storage locations, either internal or external to the core memory depending on the design of the system. The address of the job request in this storage location is then placed in its transaction item. It should be noted here that one possible location for incoming job request data might be the transaction item itself, which is an approach employed in a later example. In any event, the last operation to be carried out by the receiver is to place the transaction word for the new job request into a location (DIRQ) that then makes it available to the director function.

When the director is executed, the transaction on which it operates is available to it through the transaction word. This in turn leads it to the transaction item and then to the job request data. The director function is therefore able to analyze the job request data, determining what files are necessary, which devices are required, and the programs that will have to be loaded in order to satisfy the job request. In addition, for the programs that are to be loaded it might determine their location in the external media carrying them and the amount and kind (contiguous or noncontiguous) of memory space that will have to be allocated to them for their successful execution. All this information is entered into the transaction item, or may be entered into temporarily assigned locations, with the address of these temporary locations placed in the transaction item. The director's final operation is to move the transaction word of the job request to a location (LDRQ) that then makes it available to the loader function.

As before, the loader has access to the transaction item through the transaction word. Since the item now contains information relative to program loading, and possibly to memory and device allocation as well, these functions can be carried out at this time. Once the allocations have been made and the programs loaded into memory, a record of these allocations is placed in the job's transaction item, thereby preserving a record of the devices and units of memory allocated. In addition, after the programs called for by the job request have been loaded into their allocated positions, the location of the first instruction to be executed is stored in the transaction item as well. With the worker programs loaded into the memory for the satisfaction of the job request, the transaction becomes a member of the multiprogram set. Therefore, the last operation necessary for the loader to carry out is to move this transaction word into the list of transaction words representing programs in the multiprogram set.

The Executive Portion

As was pointed out earlier, there are two types of major actions carried out by the multiprogram executive. These are, respectively, control of order of access to the CPU, and control of order of access to the several I/O facilities of the system. We therefore consider MPX operations relative to a user transaction for each of these functions.

When MPX is operated in order to select the next program for execution, its results are characterized by selection of one of the transaction words from the list of transactions making up the multiprogram set. Possible criteria for making such a selection is a secondary consideration here, for it is clear that whatever criteria may apply, its application will result in the choice of one of the transaction words. Once the selection is made, MPX has access to the associated transaction item, and consequently to the address of the next instruction to be executed in the program that it represents. In addition, any registers that were stored when execution was interrupted have their data located in the transaction item. Therefore, MPX must also restore this data to the appropriate registers.

With these operations carried out, MPX is ready to transfer to this selected program for the continuation of its execution. However, there remains one further step to be taken relative to the transaction word. In order to distinguish the transaction word for the current operating program from all other transaction words in the multiprogram set, it is necessary to place that word into a special memory location. In Chapter 5 we have called the transaction word that appears in this location the current operating transaction, or COT, and referred to this location as the COT location of the CPU item. Thus, whenever a particular program of a job is being executed, the transaction word for that execution appears in this special memory location, the COT location. Conversely, the program executed by the COT is the current operating program, or COP.

The activities of the executive for unbuffered I/O demand multiprogramming with respect to input-output operation have been discussed in Chapters 4 and 5. In this case, the CPU transaction itself is used to represent the employment of I/O facilities. This is right so long as the execution is unbuffered, i.e., use of the CPU facility for a given execution cannot continue in parallel with use of an I/O facility for the same execution. Under buffered circumstances, however, a parallel entity derived from the CPU transaction and to be known as an I/O transaction is required. This will be introduced in Chapter 8. For the moment, suffice it to say that the execution of MPX for satisfaction of I/O requirements generated by a CPU transaction must manipulate and store either the CPU transaction or a derivative.

The Presentation Portion

We continue now with our discussion of the course of a transaction through the operating system by considering the actions of the distributor. It will be recalled that this function is used whenever a worker program generates a presentation data record. However, since each such output during an execution is associated with a CPU transaction word, the distributor has access to the necessary information relative to the presentation data, along with information about the locations in the mass storage device assigned to any previous presentation output by this execution. This information is, of course, carried in the transaction item, or is accessible through a link in the transaction item. Thus, the distributor is able to determine the memory location of the presentation data and the storage locations to which it is to be sent.

It is expected that the last presentation data record to be sent from a worker program to the distributor, destined for a particular device, will be followed by a file closing operation. This should generate an indication that the presentation data output is completed and should also cause the distributor to pass sufficient information, such as a copy of the worker transaction word, to the dispatcher function so that the user's stored presentation data can be transferred to the required presentation device. Thus, when called, the dispatcher has available to it information equivalent to a CPU transaction word representing the presence of the worker program's presentation data in the system, and may use this according to its design. In particular, it should be noted that the CPU transaction for this worker program may have long since been removed from the system by virtue of completion of the execution of its program, even though one or several presentation records still remain for handling by the dispatcher. After the dispatcher has completed the output of all presentation data associated with a particular job execution, the associated CPU transaction word can be discarded from the system, and the job is complete.

General Remarks

The foregoing discussions of the basic functions of an operating system were concerned mainly with "static" properties. It is a major thesis of this work that every operating system must include these basic functions and, in fact, can be analyzed and understood in their terms. Similarly, every operating system must record data relevant to the job being carried out for a given user, and our concept of the transaction does no more than concentrate, in a single entity, data that one often finds somewhat scattered throughout the usual operating system.

The conclusion is that thus far our basic considerations have done little more than catalogue certain operating system activities, and have established a basic information mechanism for representing the user at various positions in the system. However, when we turn our attention from the static qualities of an operating system to an investigation of some of its dynamic properties, we enter into subjects of fundamental interest; our subsequent discussions are designed to found general techniques capable of leading us to formal methods for operating system analysis.

Dynamic Interrelationships

In our foregoing description of the properties of an operating system we did not discuss the interrelationships between various operating system functions, saying only that interrelationships existed and that the connective thread, however it might be drawn, is the transaction. Furthermore, a transaction will ultimately find its way into the multiprogram set, there to be operated by the executive, and at that point represent the user in the computer system in terms of a program available for execution, i.e. a worker.

However, the various functions of the operating system that manipulate user transactions, bringing them into the system, passing them into the multiprogram set, and, through the presentation output operations, to their termination, share one property in common with the worker programs; namely, the operating system functions are themselves programs and therefore can also be represented in the computer system by transactions. This means that to initiate the action of, say, the director, it is only necessary for MPX to make the director transaction the current operating transaction. With this idea in hand we can now investigate some of the possibilities open for the dynamic interrelationships that might exist between the several operating system functions.

For example, suppose that upon notification by interrupt of the COT of the presence of a job request at the external media, MPX moves the transaction word for the receiver from a standard location R1, to a second standard location, R2 in the core memory. R1 is set to zero, and return is made to the interrupted program. When delay in the execution of a worker program causes return to MPX for redistribution of the CPU facility, it first checks the location R2 for the presence of the receiver transaction word. If present, then MPX makes this transaction word the COT, and thus allows the receiver program to be executed, bringing in the data associated with the waiting job request. The logic of these operations is summarized in Fig. 15.

Suppose now that the receiver program itself is so structured

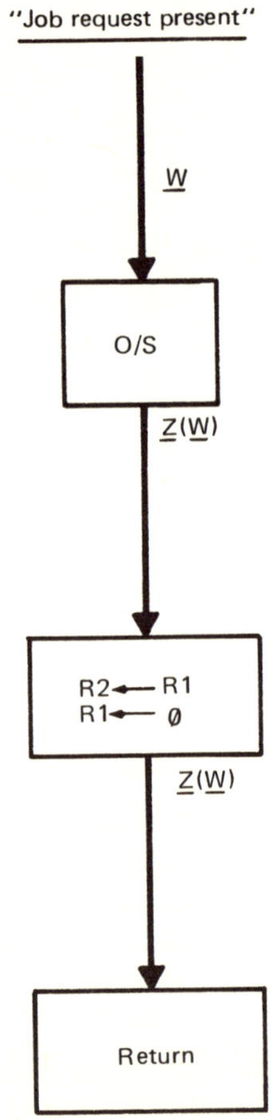

Fig. 15. Activating the Receiver

that once the job request data has been brought into the memory and validated, it is immediately passed to the director for processing. Hence, the receiver would be designed to remove its own transaction word from the COT location and place it in R1, picking up the transaction word for the director from a standard location, say D1, and placing it in the COT location, thereby causing the director to be the next program to be executed (Fig. 16). Similarly, the director, upon finishing its operations, would pick up the loader transaction and make it the current operating transaction. At termination, the loader will move its own transaction word back into a standard location, say L1, and transfer to MPX, where a new selection will be made from the multiprogram set for the next COT.

Suppose, in this hypothetical system, that the first step in the above chain has been carried out. Namely, MPX, on interrupt, has transferred the receiver transaction word from R1 to R2,

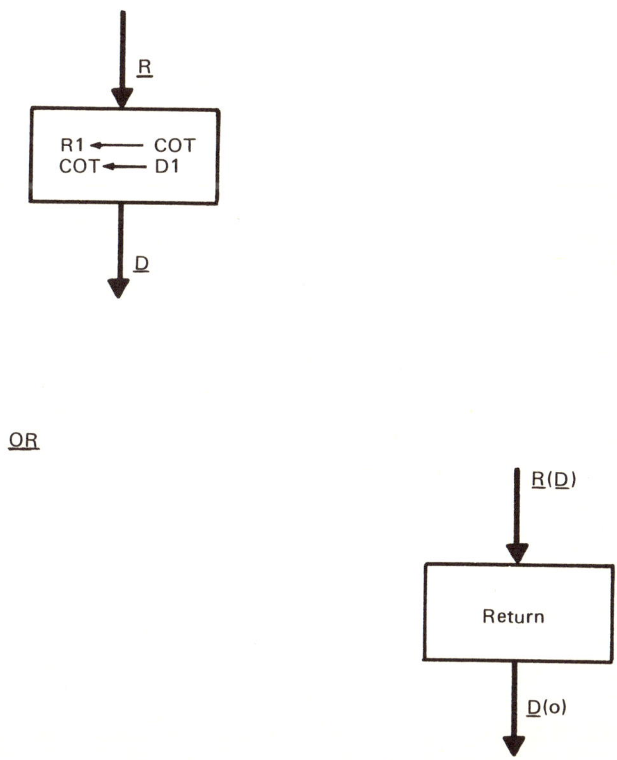

Fig. 16. Deactivating the Receiver

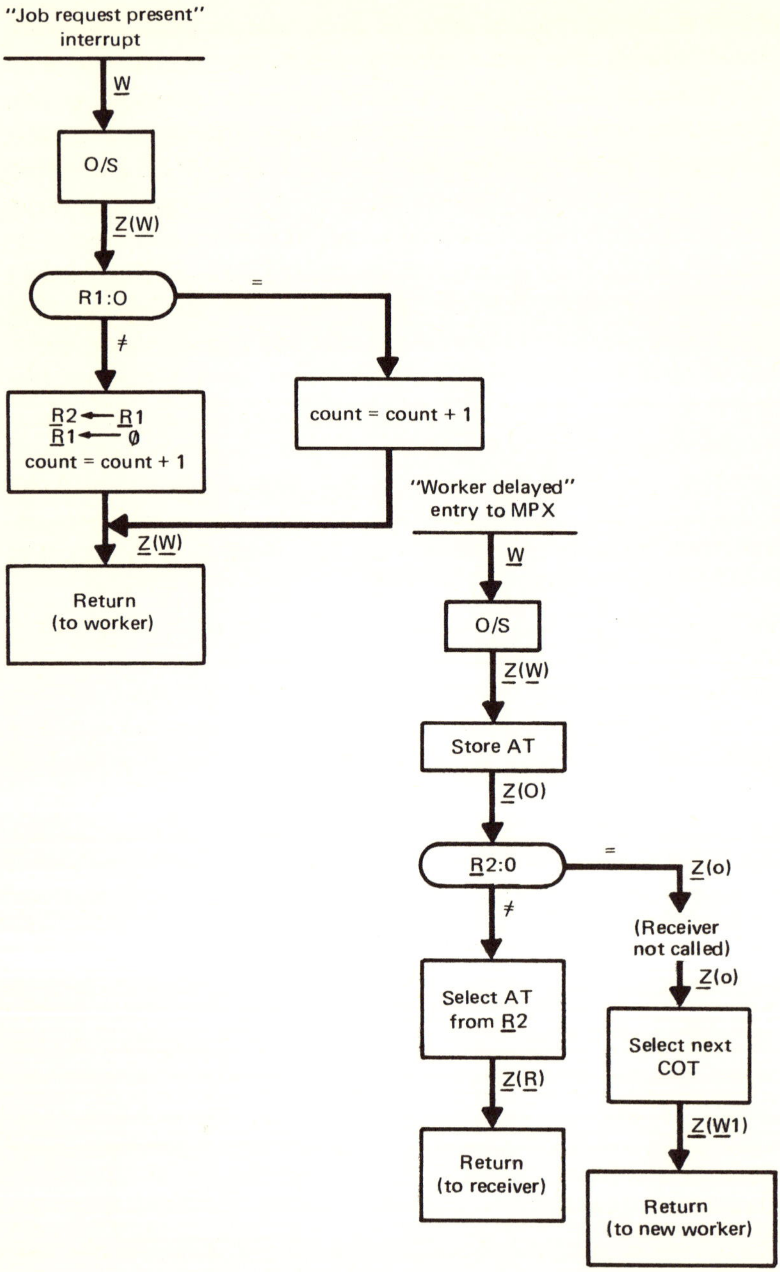

Fig. 17. Operating the Receiver in the Multipurpose Set

placed a zero in R1 and returned to the interrupted worker program. Now assume that there is a subsequent interrupt to indicate the presence of another job request on the input media. The zero contents of R1 indicate that the receiver, director, and loader (acceptance portion) are currently handling a previously received job request transaction, so that in this system, which we shall restrict to handling only one transaction at a time, the creation of a new transaction must be deferred. This can easily be accomplished by associating the location R1 with a tally count, increasing it by unity for every job request interrupt received, and decreasing it by unity each time the receiver transaction word is removed from R1 and placed into R2 (Fig. 17).

The simple system described above demonstrates a straightforward interconnection between the various functions of the operating system, i.e. each of the functions is executed sequentially in time, with the initiation of their execution occurring at the first opportunity made available by a worker program. This is the simplest of situations; in the next paragraph we suggest the most complex interrelationship but pass over it quickly, deferring amplification to the example of the next chapter.

Consider then a multiprogram set that contains not only the transaction words for each of the worker programs represented in the system, but which in addition contains transaction words for each of the acceptance functions. That is, augmenting the transaction words for each of the worker programs in the multiprogram set are the transaction words for the receiver, director, and loader. This means that whatever criteria are applied by MPX to the multiprogram set in selection of the transaction word to next appear as COT is also applied to the transaction words representing these acceptance programs. Hence, whatever degree of multiprogramming is achieved among the worker programs is thereby extended to these elements of the operating system. The result is what we shall refer to as the *multiprogrammed* operating system.

Having come this far, it is clearly a simple step to add the transaction words for the presentation functions, distributor and dispatcher, to the multiprogram set. The result is operating systems with very surprising qualities.

CHAPTER 7

AN OPERATING SYSTEM FOR UNBUFFERED EXECUTIONS

Introduction

IN CHAPTER 4, it was demonstrated that the center of the operating system, the multiprogram executive, is completely determined by the constraint that all programs executing under its control operate their I/O activities on an unbuffered basis. This constraint then defines a set of states for worker programs that are mutually exclusive, i.e. a program may be in one and only one state at any time during its execution. From these assumed and derived conditions, it was a relatively easy matter to determine the logical structure of the multiprogram executive. Chapter 5 was then devoted to the development of the transaction concept, and to techniques leading to the method of transaction analysis, concluding with a review of the MPX for the unbuffered case in transaction chart form. In the present chapter, we apply the transaction method to the development of a complete operating system that includes all of the necessary functions discussed in Chapter 6.

The developments thus far have, in general, dwelled on certain data and function definitions as they pertain to the operating system, and in a general way, on the problem of operating system structure. In the preceding chapters, a more detailed analysis of only the MPX for the unbuffered case was considered. It was important to note for this case, however, that though the MPX is essentially constrained to having the logical structure indicated, the general shape of the operating system and its overall performance are dependent on the design of its acceptance and presentation portions. That is to say, within the constraint that all programs implementing the acceptance and presentation functions in the operating system execute unbuffered I/O, both their functional activities, i.e. what they do, and their structural relationships are open to design.

Thus, it is clear that though the center of the operating system, the MPX, is fixed logically by the unbuffered assumption, the overall operating system can be formulated to satisfy the application needs of a particular installation environment. It is the purpose of this chapter to define such an environment as an example and then to develop a complete operating system that will satisfy its requirements. The system developed will be completely multiprogrammed with all programs implementing acceptance and presentation functions as members of the multiprogram set. The method of the presentation will be by means of transaction analysis.

The Problem Environment

In order to have a design objective, it is necessary to determine the requirements of the operating environment that must be satisfied by the operating system overall. For the purpose of the present example, the following environmental requirements are therefore assumed.

Job requests come to the operating system via a card reader. These requests may be for the execution of already compiled programs or for the compilation of programs in source code format. The problem requires that all initial inputs to worker programs come from high speed initial input devices, such as magnetic tapes or disk packs. In the event that an initial input is originally in card format, the system must therefore provide a card-to-device function.

It is assumed that the compilation activity in the environment is sufficiently high to require a reentrant compiler. On the other hand, the frequency of compilation is not high enough to justify permanent core residency for the compiler program. Therefore, the compiler is to be treated as a worker program that is loaded when required and used as a reentrant program for subsequent requirements that arrive during its core residency.

A similar condition exists relative to the requirements of the card-to-device function, so that the program implementing this function is resident in core for only the duration of its execution. Thus, the environment requires that both the compiler and the card-to-device programs be considered as worker programs by the operating system.

It is finally assumed for this problem that a high printing volume is expected. Therefore, as will be noted below, there will be two-on-line printers available, and it is a requirement on the system to operate these at a maximum throughput efficiency in the context of multiple access by a number of worker programs.

Hardware Configuration

For the purpose of this example, it is assumed that the single CPU and memory are connected to two card readers, two printers, and a disk, as a minimum. These devices are to serve the needs of the various functions of the operating system. In addition, there may be tapes and mass storage devices providing external storage capacity for meeting the needs of worker programs.

In the following paragraphs, a broad overview of the several functions of the operating system is presented. This is then followed by a complete transaction analysis.

Acceptance Portions

Of the two card readers available on the system, one of them (reader #1) will be designated for the receipt of job requests. It is assumed that the presence of new job request data on this reader is made known to the operating system via an alert interrupt that will be handled by MPX. Recognizing this interrupt as one which designates the presence of the job request on reader #1, MPX will create a new transaction to represent the incoming user. This transaction will consist of both a transaction item and a transaction word, as described in Chapter 5. In the case of the transaction item, MPX simply makes available the space that is required, with specific information to be filled in as it is developed during the course of the transaction through the acceptance portion of the operating system. The transaction word that is created contains the name of the transaction item. This means that the information in the transaction word is the address of the newly created transaction item's location in the memory. MPX then places the new transaction word onto a queue of such transaction words that are available to the receiver. This will be referred to as the receiver queue, or RCVQ. Finally, MPX determines whether or not the receiver is active, and if not, activates the receiver by placing its transaction word *R*, onto the AQ.

When active, the receiver will select a transaction word from the RCVQ. It will then read job request data from reader #1 into the locations assigned to the transaction item associated with the selected transaction. Thus, the first application of the transaction item is as storage for the incoming job request data.

The next operation of the receiver is to place the transaction word for the message just received into a queue of such transaction words that are associated with the director. This will be referred to as the director queue, or DIRQ. The final function of the receiver is to activate the director if it is currently not busy.

When the director is executed it selects a transaction word from the DIRQ. This transaction word contains the address of its associated transaction item, which in turn contains the job request data that has been received for this transaction. The job request is then interpreted by the director, allowing it to determine whether a card-to-device activity, compilation, or general worker program execution is required.

If a card-to-device action is indicated, then the execution of that program is instituted much the same as if it were a general worker program. If the job request indicates that compilation is required, then the present transaction word representing the user is associated with a generic transaction for the compiler program with the resultant combination being used to execute the compiler. The technique employed will be shown in detail below. The further consideration relative to a job request for compilation is whether or not the compiler is currently resident in the memory. If it is resident in memory, then its execution is effected immediately for this transaction since the compiler is reentrant, by simply placing the combined transaction word into the availability queue. On the other hand, if the compiler is nonresident at this time, the transaction is treated as if it were for a general worker program.

The director functions for handling general worker programs are designed to determine if the devices required, as interpreted from the job request, are available for assignment. If sufficient devices are not available, then the transaction word for the worker program is placed into a director list, and a notation of the required devices is made. The transaction will remain in this list until program terminations by other transactions have freed sufficient devices to make its own execution possible. When the devices required by a transaction become available, the transaction is placed into a queue associated with the loader. This will be referred to as the LDRQ. The director then ascertains whether or not the loader is active, and if it is not active, makes it so.

The execution of the loader program causes it to select a transaction word from the LDRQ. For the purposes of the present example, transaction words are ordered in the queue on the basis of core memory requirement, with the transaction having the largest memory requirement having the highest priority. The loader next determines if the memory required can be allocated, and if not, the transaction is returned to the LDRQ. The loader is then made inactive until the next program termination, at which time it will be activated again by MPX. In this fashion, programs with the largest memory requirement will not have their execution indefinitely deferred. This is particularly applicable to the problem environment under consideration since a relatively high compiler utilization is expected, and it is likely that this will be one of the larger programs using the system.

In the event that memory can be allocated, the allocation process is carried out with the memory assignment being stored in the transaction item associated with the transaction word of current interest to the loader. The required program is then loaded, and when loading is complete the transaction word for the newly loaded program is placed on the availability queue. In this fashion, the worker program becomes a member of the multiprogram set.

The Presentation Portion

The computer system has available two on-line printers and the system disk so that in order to achieve an effective presentation portion, the operating system will consist of a distributor program and a dispatcher program.

The distributor accepts inputs from the members of the multiprogram set that are destined for output on a printer. This data is organized by worker program into a printer buffer on the operating system disk. The distributor operations are activated by an I/O call, designated for printer output, to MPX. MPX then places the transaction word associated with the calling program on a queue belonging to the distributor. This will be referred to as the DTRQ. MPX then activates the distributor if it is not already busy.

When executed, the distributor selects a transaction word from DTRQ, places the record destined for the printer in a block of such records for this worker program, and, when the block is full, places that block into the printer buffer on the disk. However, whether or not the emplacement of a current record into a block fills that block, the transaction making the call to output to the printer is then placed back into the availability queue, from whence it may continue its execution.

The dispatcher program is a reentrant code that is associated with two transactions, one for each of the two printers. These transactions are activated upon termination of a worker program, which occurs within MPX. On this occasion, the transaction word for the terminating worker program is placed on the dispatcher queue, DSPQ. The termination function within MPX then determines if one of the two dispatcher transactions is inactive, and if so, activates that transaction.

When the execution of the dispatcher program is initiated, it selects a transaction word from DSPQ. It then locates the first block of data to be printed for this transaction in the printer buffer on the disk and brings that block into the memory. Records are then printed from this block until the block is empty, at which time the next block for printing is brought in from the printer buffer. The cycle is repeated until all blocks associated with this transaction have been output to the printer, after which, operations by the system on behalf of the worker transaction have been completed and therefore the transaction can be destroyed.

The MPX

The multiprogram executive for this operating system is essentially that described in Chapter 4 and again in Chapter 5. Since the execution of all acceptance, presentation, and worker programs is on an unbuffered I/O basis, variations in MPX are due mainly to special requirements of the director, loader, distributor, and dispatcher functions.

In the case of the director, it may be necessary to defer the passing of a worker transaction to the loader for further action due to the unavailability of peripheral devices. Therefore, it is incumbent upon the multiprogram executive in its program termination portion to review the device availability in light of peripheral devices released by terminating worker programs. Transactions that have been set aside by the director until devices have become available are then placed again into the DIRQ by this portion of MPX.

The memory allocation function is associated with the loader. As indicated earlier, transactions are selected in descending order of core memory requirement, with successful allocation for the transaction with the largest requirement necessary before any further allocation and loading can be carried out. Therefore, in the event that an allocation cannot be obtained for a given transaction, it is necessary for the further execution of the loader to be deferred until sufficient terminations have occurred to supply the required memory space. It is therefore a function of the termination portion of MPX to investigate whether or not further execution of the Loader has been deferred for this reason. In the event that the further execution of the Loader has been deferred, it is reactivated by this portion of MPX.

As mentioned earlier, it is necessary for MPX to determine if an I/O call is for output of data destined for the printer. The functions for MPX in such an event are to ascertain whether or not the distributor is active, and to activate it if not. It is also necessary for MPX to place the transaction word for the outputting worker program into the distributor queue.

The presentation of printer output from a given worker program is not initiated until that program has called on the termination portion of MPX, indicating that it has completed all of its required computations. When this occurs, it is necessary for the termination portion of MPX to activate one of the currently inactive dispatcher transactions, if there is such, and to place the transaction word for the terminating worker program into the dispatcher queue.

The Transaction Chart

With the foregoing broad description of the operating system, attention is now given to elements of this system in somewhat greater detail. The method used is that of transaction analysis, introduced in Chapter 5, so that for each operating system program which is to execute as an independent asynchronous function there will be associated a unique transaction word and transaction item. With this technique then, each of the transaction charts will indicate the current operating transaction as being that transaction word associated with the particular operating system program. The charts will also show specific transaction words of interest at various points in the logic of the transaction charts. These will appear as available transactions in the transaction term.

Programs of the operating system are said to be "independent" when the program is associated with its own transaction (or transactions, in the case of the dispatcher) and "asynchronous" if the transaction is as well a member of the multiprogrammed set. Programs that are capable of executing under such conditions can therefore be described independently of one another, with interface interdependence among such programs relegated to certain specified queues, and data contained in transaction items. In short, such programs are expositionally and operationally independent of one another up to, and including, their individual transaction items.

The Receiver

As a program, the receiver has its own transaction word and transaction item. The location in the memory of the transaction item for receiver will be at symbolic location *R*, and this location in turn will be the identification for the transaction item and therefore will appear as the symbol for the receiver's transaction word. In addition, there is a fixed location in the memory, whose symbolic address will be designated as R1, containing the transaction word for the receiver program when that program is inactive. These two elements of the receiver program and their symbolic locations in the core memory are shown in schematic form in Fig. 18.

The general sequence of events for introducing a job request into the system is for the job request data containing function and parameter specifications to be loaded onto card reader #1, after which a manually operated alert interrupt is signaled to the operating system by the operator. This interrupt is received by MPX and interpreted as meaning that job request data is present at the card reader. The job request is the user's representation to the system of the actions that he seeks from it. On the other hand, the transaction is the system's representation of the user's presence in the system, from job request through its processing into loaded programs, the execution of those programs, and the final output of any presentation data. Therefore, upon receipt of the alert, or job request interrupt, MPX will create a new transaction representing this yet to be received job request.

The creation of a transaction for this user involves the establishment of a transaction item in the core memory at some particular location, and the use of that address as the transaction word. With the transaction item and transaction word established for the new job request, MPX now makes the transaction word available to the receiver. This is accomplished by placing the

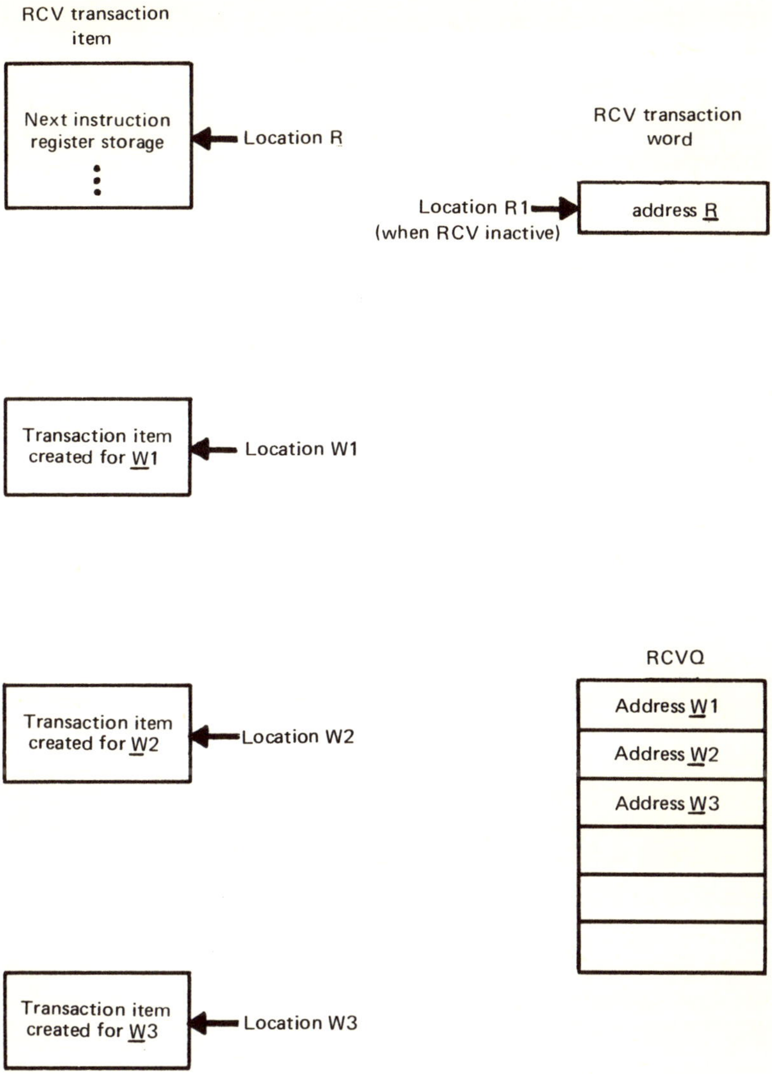

Fig. 18. Transactions and the RCVQ

newly created transaction word into the receiver queue, RCVQ, with its position in that queue based on time of receipt.

The above described process is general for the receipt of all job requests placed on the card reader and whose presence is signaled by the alert interrupt to MPX. The operations described are independent of the asynchronous operations of the receiver itself. Thus, as the receiver executes its functions relative to one of the transactions in its receiver queue, that execution may be interrupted due to the presence of a new job request on the card reader. From the receiver's point of view, it is totally unaware of the occurrence of such interrupts. Since all of its subsequent actions are generated by the presence of transaction words in its RCVQ, the asynchronous emplacement of transaction words into this queue by MPX has no effect on the receiver's actions, other than to continue its operations.

The diagram of Fig. 18 indicates the situation where three user transactions have been created for job requests awaiting action at the card reader. The transaction items are shown in symbolic locations *W*1, *W*2 and *W*3, and their corresponding transaction words appear in the RCVQ. With this situation, the activation of the receiver is accomplished by MPX, placing the receiver transaction word into the availability queue, thus making it available for execution. When the execution of the receiver is initiated, it will select the top transaction word from RCVQ, read the corresponding job request data, carry out subsequent actions, as will be noted below, and finally check RCVQ to see if it is empty. If not empty, it will return to its initial address and continue its execution relative to the next transaction word in the queue. This cycle of operations is continued until RCVQ is emptied. In the course of the cycle, as mentioned earlier, the queue may be asynchronously filled by action of the MPX in response to an alert interrupt, signaling the presence of an additional job request at the card reader.

The structure of the transaction item for the newly created transaction prior to its processing by the receiver is shown in Fig. 19. As indicated there, MPX has placed the time of receipt

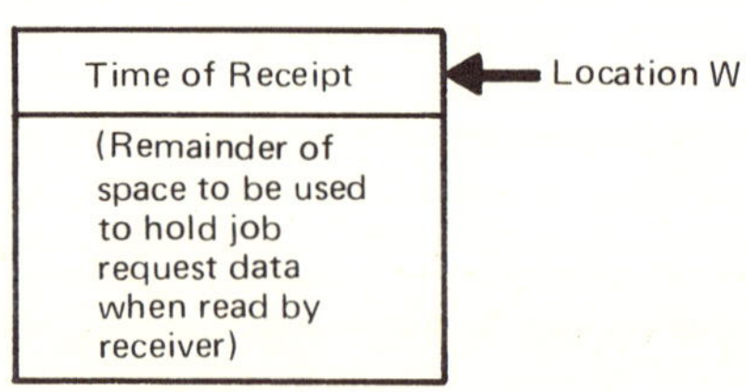

Fig. 19. Transaction Item for a New Transaction

of the alert interrupt into the transaction item. The remainder space in the transaction item is empty and will be used as the location into which the corresponding job request is read by the receiver.

The transaction chart for the receiver program is shown in Fig. 20. The receiver is activated by MPX when its transaction word is placed onto the availability queue. When the receiver is selected as current operating program, its transaction word is removed from the AQ and placed into the COT location of the CPU item. The symbolic name of the receiver transaction is *R*, and therefore will appear as such in the transaction chart.

The execution of the receiver is initiated at connector 1 in Fig. 20. Since the current operating program is the receiver, the current operating transaction (the COT) is the receiver transaction *R*. There is no available transaction of interest to the receiver at this point. At box 1, the first action of the receiver is to select an available transaction from the receiver queue. This will be a transaction word for a newly created user transaction. At the completion of this operation, the transaction term is as indicated upon exit from box 1. This shows that *R* is the current operating transaction and that the selected user transaction, *W*, is the available transaction of interest to the receiver at this point.

The next action of the receiver (box 2) is to read the job request data corresponding to the user transaction. The core memory locations to be used for receiving the job request data are those locations assigned to the transaction item for this user transaction. The transaction word, *W*, is actually the address of this transaction item, so that in executing the function of box 2, the receiver has available all necessary information to designate the input locations for the card reading operation.

Implicit to the execution of the function in box 2 is an I/O operation for input. The execution of this I/O operation will be carried out by the I/O package within MPX, during the course of which MPX will treat the receiver program as it does all other programs under its control. Therefore, the receiver transaction, *R*, calls MPX at its I/O call entrance and passes through the initiation queue associated with the channel connected to the card reader. In its turn, this transaction will be given access

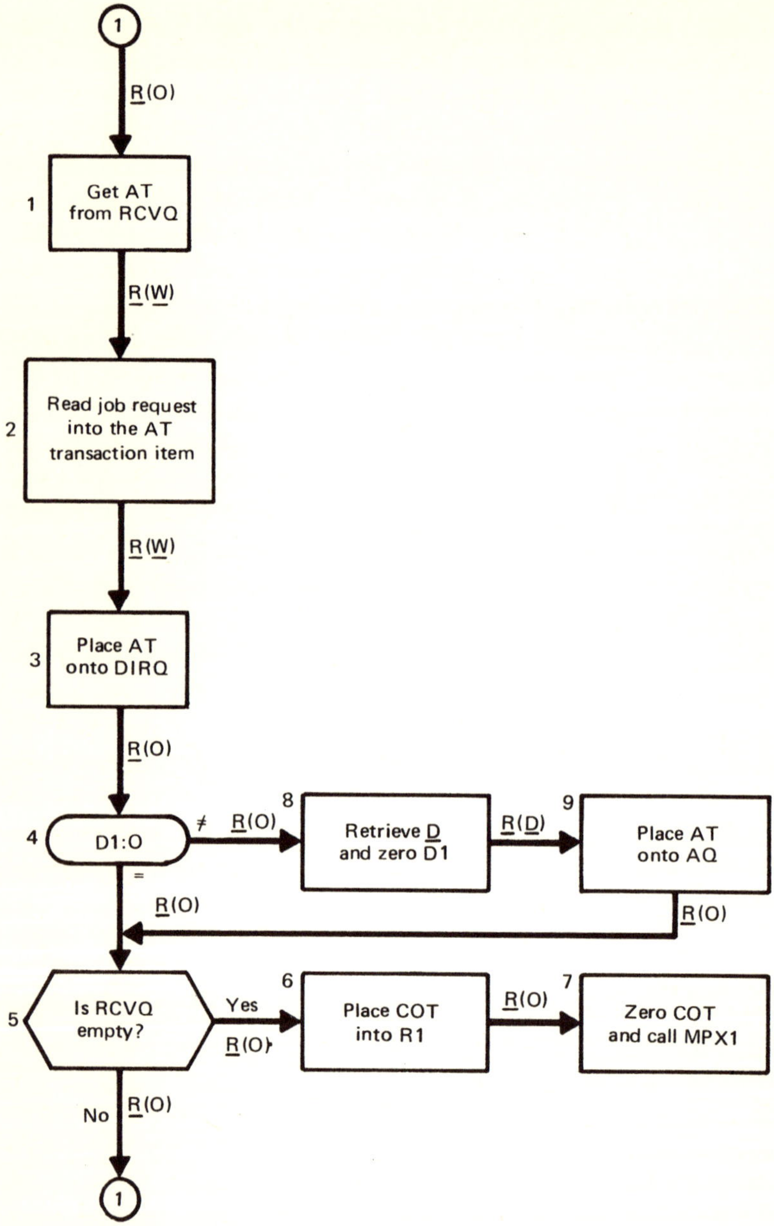

Fig. 20. Transaction Chart for Receiver Program

to the channel, and for the duration of the card read will reside in the associated reference list word for that channel.

For the duration of this hiatus into the operating system the receiver transaction cannot appear in the AQ, and therefore the receiver program is not available for further execution. When the job request is complete, however, its transaction word, *R*, will appear in the AQ and will subsequently be selected as COT. This will cause a return to the operations of box 2, from which point the receiver will resume its execution.

Immediately prior to the transfer of *R* into MPX for accomplishing the card input function, the transaction word, *W*, in the AT location of the CPU item, is safe-stored. This word is then retrieved on return from MPX once *R* has been reinstituted as current operating transaction. Thus on entering box 3, the CPU term indicates that the newly created transaction, *W*, of earlier interest to *R*, remains as its available transaction.

On entrance to box 3, the job request data for the user transaction, *W*, resides in the associated transaction item for *W*. The next action required on behalf of this transaction is to notify the director of its presence and the need for the attention of that function. This is accomplished at box 3 by placing the available transaction onto the director queue, DIRQ. The director, operating on lines similar to that for the receiver, will carry out its functions for each of the transactions that it finds in the DIRQ, and therefore it will eventually get to the transaction just placed there by the receiver.

Once the AT has been placed onto DIRQ, there is no longer an available transaction for *R*, as indicated by the CPU term on exit from box 3. At box 4, the receiver determines whether or not the director is active. If the director is inactive, then the director transaction, *D*, is to be found in the symbolic core memory location D1. If active, however, the director transaction will be a member of the multiprogrammed set and therefore is in one of the queues or lists under the control of MPX. In this case, the symbolic location D1 will be empty. Assume that this latter case applies so that the test at box 4 leads directly to box 5, with the AT still zero for the transaction *R*. At box 5, the transaction determines whether or not the receiver queue is empty.

If it is not empty, then it contains at least one additional user transaction to be treated by the receiver program. Note that the CPU term at exit from box 5 remains *R*(O), which is the condition for entry to connector 1 for reiterating the execution of the receiver.

Returning to box 5, in the event that the receiver queue is empty at this test, then the next operations accomplished by the transaction, *R*, are designed to deactivate it, since there is no further requirement for its execution by newly created transactions. Hence, at box 6 the receiver places the COT into the location R1. This has the effect of moving the receiver transaction, *R*, out of the CPU item as current operating transaction and into the standard location for the receiver's transaction, its presence in which indicates to MPX that the receiver is inactive. As indicated in the transaction chart, both on entry and exit from box 6, there is no available transaction. The final operation in the receiver is to place zeros in the current operating transaction location and to call MPX at a special entrance location, MPX1, the significance of which will become apparent in later discussions.

In the event that the receiver finds the director inactive after the new transaction has been placed on DIRQ, the location D1 will contain the director's transaction and hence will be nonzero. Therefore the receiver, with the AT location of the CPU item remaining empty, will transfer to box 8. At this point, the receiver picks up the director transaction from the location D1 and replaces the contents of that location with zeros, thus indicating on any subsequent test that the director is busy. Now the director transaction, *D*, is the transaction available to the receiver transaction, *R*, for manipulation. It therefore appears in the AT location of the CPU item. In box 9, therefore, the activation of the director is completed by placing the AT onto the availability queue, from whence it will be selected in due course by MPX for execution. This operation, having moved the director transaction from the AT location to the AQ, leaves the AT empty, as indicated in the CPU term on exit from box 9.

Having activated the director, the receiver now transfers to box 5 in its transaction chart where it makes the aforementioned test regarding the content of the RCVQ and proceeds as previously described.

It is important to note in the above description of the receiver program that the major items of logical interest in its design are the manipulation of the newly created user transaction and the director transaction when necessary. These transaction words are effectively indirect addresses to the associated transaction items, so that the receiver has access to all information necessary to the operations it has to carry out. More important, however, is the fact that the operation of the receiver is totally asynchronous with the operations of the director or any other acceptance, presentation, or worker program in the multiprogrammed set. Furthermore, its functions are executed asynchronously with respect to MPX as well, this latter function asynchronously creating transaction items and transaction words for new job requests and placing them into the RCVQ. This may be thought of as being accomplished in the background of the receiver's execution, so that the receiver functions relative to transaction words it discovers in RCVQ without concern as to either the timing or method of arrival of these transactions in that queue.

The Director

As in the case of the receiver, transaction words appear in the director queue (DIRQ) asynchronously with the operation of both the director and the remainder of the operating system. The transactions that appear in DIRQ arrive there by virtue of receiver actions, as described earlier. When the director is activated, its transaction word is placed by the receiver into the availability queue. It is thus made eligible for selection by MPX as COT, at which point the execution of the director program will be initiated at connector 1 in the transaction chart of Fig. 21. When the director is executed, its transaction, *D*, is the current operating transaction in the COT location of the CPU item, and the AT location of the CPU item is empty. Therefore, the CPU term is as shown in Fig. 21 at connector 1.

The Director has been activated because there is at least one transaction word, representing a received job request, on DIRQ, and its operation at box 1 is to pick the first transaction word

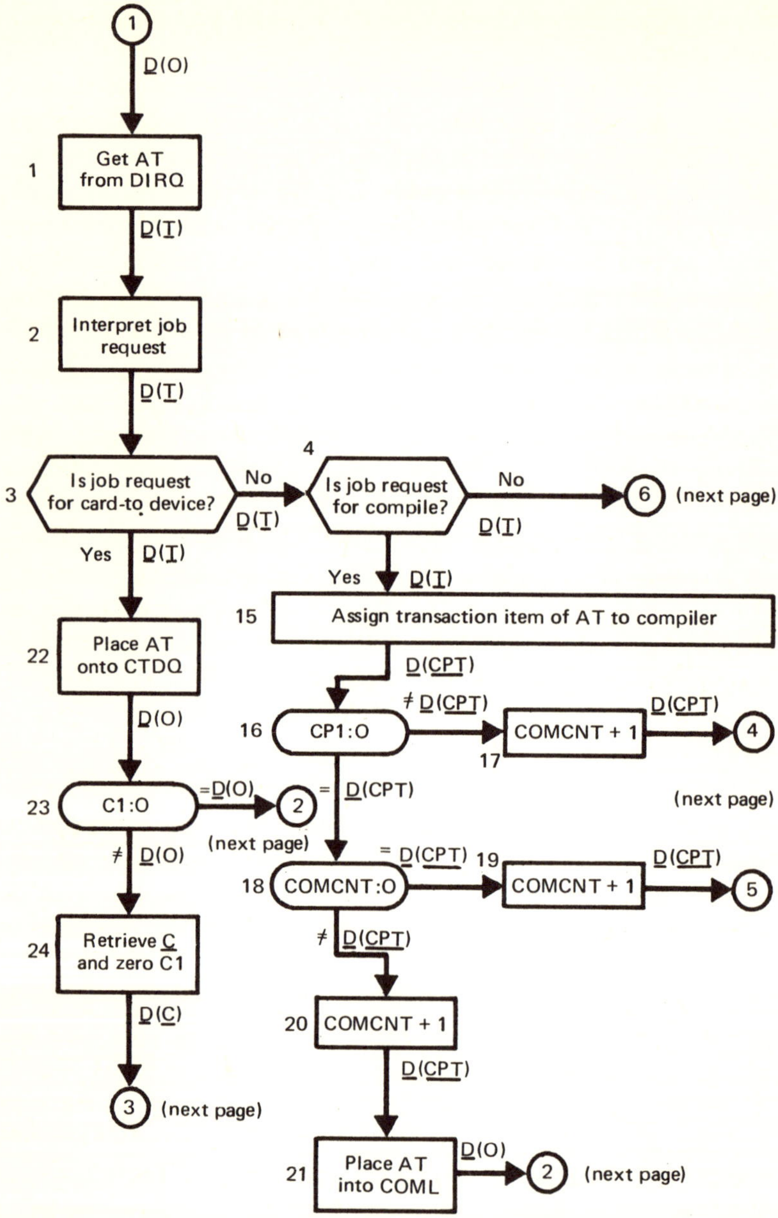
1
D(O)
1 Get AT from DIRQ
D(T)
2 Interpret job request
D(T)
3 Is job request for card-to device?
No
D(T)
4 Is job request for compile?
No
D(T)
6 (next page)
Yes D(T)
Yes D(T)
15 Assign transaction item of AT to compiler
D(CPT)
22 Place AT onto CTDQ
D(O)
16 CP1:O
≠ D(CPT)
17 COMCNT + 1
D(CPT)
4 (next page)
= D(CPT)
23 C1:O
= D(O)
2 (next page)
≠ D(O)
18 COMCNT:O
= D(CPT)
19 COMCNT + 1
D(CPT)
5
24 Retrieve C and zero C1
D(C)
3 (next page)
≠ D(CPT)
20 COMCNT + 1
D(CPT)
21 Place AT into COML
D(O)
2 (next page)

Fig. 21. DIR

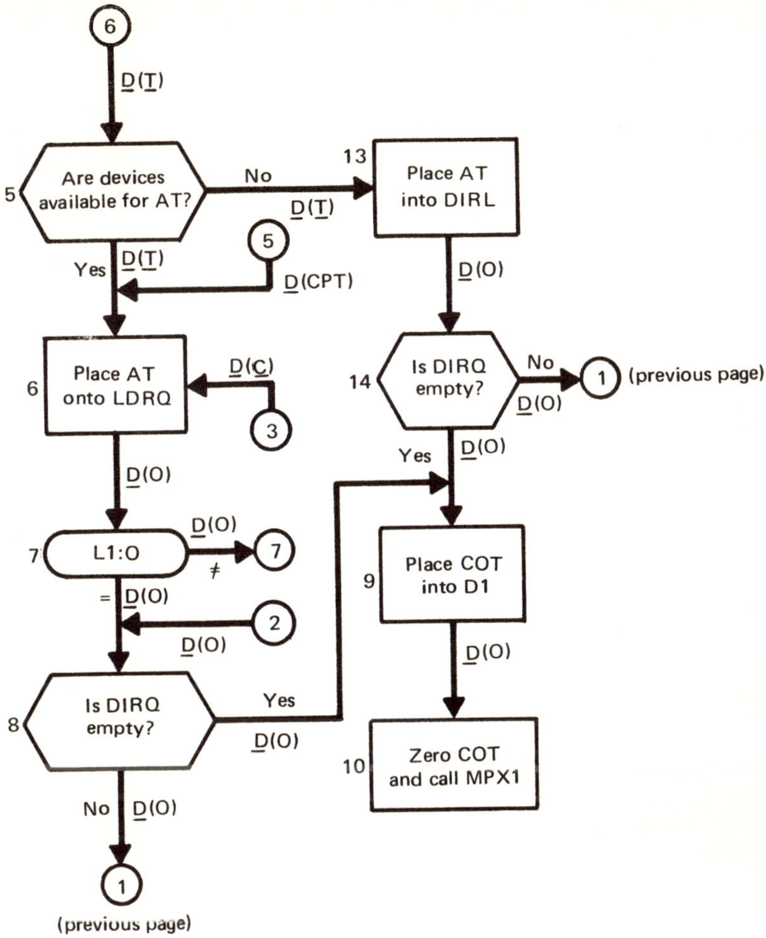

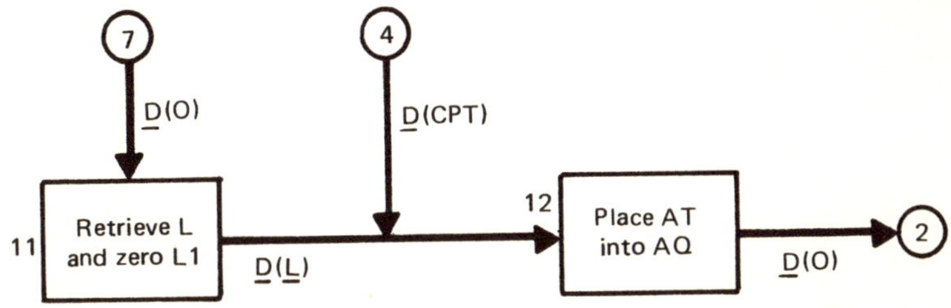

Fig. 21. Continued

from DIRQ, placing that word into the AT location of the CPU item. The transaction thus made available for manipulation by the director is indicated generically by the symbol T, as shown in the CPU term on exit from box 1.

It is the job of the director program to ascertain whether the available transaction is for a card-to-device operation, a compilation, or other execution. The purpose of box 2, therefore, is to represent the interpretation of the job request data located in the transaction item of the available transaction. In box 3, the intent of the job request is queried. Assuming that it is not for a card-to-device operation, then the available transaction, along with the director's transaction in the CPU item, transfers to box 4 to determine if the job request is for a compilation. Again, assume that the job request is for other than a compile, so that transfer is made to connector 6 of the second chart of Fig. 21.

At this point, it has been ascertained by the director program that the transaction it is now treating is for an execution other than card-to-device or compile. Therefore, at box 5, the director determines if the required peripheral devices (as determined by the interpretation at box 2) are available for the AT at this time. If the answer is affirmative, then transfer is made to box 6 where the AT (the transaction T, of current interest to the director) is placed onto the loader queue. Thus, at the completion of the execution of box 6, the director has determined that the transaction for which it is currently executing is for other than a card-to-device, or compile operation, and that the peripheral devices required for this execution are available for assignment. Hence, at box 6 the transaction for this execution is placed into the loader queue (LDRQ) for loading of the required programs, and subsequent execution. Having accomplished this, the director no longer has an available transaction, as indicated by the CPU term on exit from box 6. However, since the director has placed the transaction word into the loader queue, it is necessary for it to ascertain whether or not the loader is currently active. This is the function of box 7. When the loader is inactive, the transaction word for the loader will be located in a core memory location the symbolic address of which is designated as L1.

Hence, if the contents of L1 are equal to zero, the loader is active and is present somewhere within the multiprogrammed set In this case, therefore, the director proceeds to box 8 since it has no further operations relative to the initiation of loading for the transaction of current interest.

At box 8, the director tests whether or not there exists an additional transaction word in the DIRQ for its attention. If this queue is not empty, then the transaction word found at the top indicates the presence of a further job request requiring treatment by the director. In this case therefore, the director transfers to connector 1 of Fig. 21, to repeat the above operations. Note that at this point the CPU term indicates that the AT location is empty.

If the director queue contains no further transaction words for worker programs requiring interpretation, then transfer is made to box 9 of the second chart of Fig. 21. At this point the director has no further actions to carry out, and, therefore, it will deactivate itself by placing its transaction word into the location D1, where its presence there indicates to the receiver program the current inactivity of the director. These operations are indicated at box 9, where the director transaction, currently located in the CPU item in the COT location, is placed into the symbolic location D1. The next operation at box 10 makes the contents of the COT zero and calls MPX1, indicating the temporary termination of an operating system program.

Returning now to box 7, assume that having placed the worker transaction of current interest into the loader queue, the director now finds the loader inactive. This is determined by the contents of symbolic location L1 being nonzero, in which case this location actually contains the loader transaction word. Under these circumstances, the director transfers to connector 7 of this chart, with the CPU term as shown. This is an entry to box 11, where the loader transaction, *L*, is retrieved from the location L1, and that location is reset to zero to indicate that the loader is now active. Note that the available transaction is now the loader transaction and the director's next operation is at box 12 where the available transaction (the loader transaction) is placed onto the AQ. This completes the activation of the loader.

On exit from box 12, the CPU term properly indicates that there is no longer a transaction of current interest. This is the proper form of the CPU term for transfer to connector 2, at which entry the decision as to whether the director should continue or terminate is executed.

In the sequence of operations for a worker program requiring other than a card-to-device or compile operation, it is possible that the devices required by that program are not available at this time. Therefore, at box 5 of the second chart of Fig. 21 transfer is made to box 13. At this point, the worker transaction *T* (the available transaction) has insufficient devices available for the initiation of its execution. Hence, the available transaction is placed into a list (DIRL) within the director where it will remain until a worker termination occurs, at which time sufficient devices may be released to allow assignment to this transaction. Thus, further activities on the part of the director for this transaction, *T*, are deferred until a subsequent worker program termination.

Since at box 13 the director places the available transaction into a list, there is no longer a transaction of interest, as indicated by the CPU term on exit from box 13. Under this condition then, the director enters the functions of box 14 where it determines whether the director queue DIRQ, is empty. In the case where the queue is not empty, there exists a further worker transaction seeking service by the director and transfer is made to connector 1 of the first chart of Fig. 21 with the CPU term as shown.

On the other hand, if the director queue contains no further transaction words seeking the attention of the director, transfer is made to box 9, where the director places its own transaction word into its inactive location, D1, sets the COT location to zero (box 10), and transfers to MPX1 for its termination.

Thus far we have considered the case where the transaction, *T*, being treated by the director, represents a job request for other than a card-to-device or compile operation. We consider now the case (box 4) where the job request is for compilation of a source code program. At this point the director transaction

D, transfers to box 15 with the transaction representing the compilation request as the available transaction.

As mentioned earlier, the compiler program is in the first place a reentrant code, and in the second treated as a worker program. It is necessary at this point to alloy the transaction seeking compilation service with the compiler program itself. Therefore, the available transaction, *T*, is assigned as the transaction for execution of the compiler. This means no more than indicating in the transaction item that the name of the program which it will execute is the name of the compiler program (whether the compiler program is resident in core memory or not will be discussed below). Thus, executions of the compiler program are done on the basis of the transaction allocated to the job request, which uses the compiler program as a "service."

On exit from box 15, therefore, the current transaction of interest (the available transaction) is indicated as the transaction word for the compiler program. This is taken generically (for all reentrant calls on the compiler) as the transaction CPT. Thus the transaction term, on exit from 15, indicates that the available transaction is CPT.

The director's next action is associated with the core residency of the compiler. A switch, CP1, is used to designate the presence or absence of the compiler program, with that switch set when the compiler is resident in core memory, and zero otherwise. Assume that the compiler is resident (CP1 not equal to zero) at box 16. Therefore, the director transfers to box 17 where the counter COMCNT is incremented by unity. This COMCNT indicates, at any time, the number of transactions concurrently executing the compiler program and is necessary for determining when the presence of compiler program in the memory can be terminated. With this count incremented, the director transaction transfers to connector 4 of the second chart of Fig. 21. This is an entrance to box 12. Since the compiler program is resident in core memory (CP1 nonzero), and because the compiler program is reentrant code, it can be executed directly. Therefore, the current transaction now set as a transaction for executing the compiler program is placed into the availability queue at box 12, from which it will be ultimately selected as the COT by MPX.

On exit from box 12, the available transaction location of the CPU item is empty, since this transaction is now in the availability queue, and transfer is made to connector 2 as an entrance to box 8.

Returning now to box 16, assume that the switch CP1 is equal to zero. In this case, the compiler is not core resident and therefore one of two conditions prevails. In the first place, the compiler program may have been "rolled-out" (its space made available for other allocations) and therefore the present transaction will be used to create a call on the loader for reloading of the compiler into the core memory. On the other hand, a previous transaction may have been used for this purpose, so that the compiler program is in the process of being loaded at this time. In this case, the director will store worker transactions seeking to execute the compiler until the loading of the compiler program has been completed.

Box 18 is the point at which the director ascertains whether or not a copy of the compiler is currently in the process of being loaded. This is accomplished by checking the value of the counter COMCNT. Since the compiler is not in core (CP1 equals zero), if COMCNT is equal to zero then no previous worker transaction has initiated the loading of the compiler program. Therefore, the director with CPT (a compiler transaction) as the AT transfers to box 19 where the count of the number of programs seeking the compiler's service is incremented by unity, after which transfer to connector 5 of the second chart of Fig. 21 is made.

Execution at connector 5 with the available transaction, CPT, is an entrance to box 6, at which point the director places the available transaction onto the loader queue and thus inaugurates the loading of a program (in this case the compiler) into the core memory. The following operations at boxes 7, 8, etc., have been described earlier and determine whether or not the loader is currently busy and if the director should continue its execution for remaining transactions in DIRQ.

Returning to box 18, consider the case where a previous transaction has found the compiler noncore resident and has therefore, as above described, been used to inaugurate its loading. At the present time, for the current transaction, this loading has yet to be completed. In this case, though CP1 is still equal to zero, the value of COMCNT will be nonzero since the previous transaction has incremented its value by unity. In this case, the director transfers to box 20, where the count of worker transactions that are seeking access to the compiler is incremented, and then transfers to box 21 where this worker transaction is placed into the list COML. The list COML is used as a temporary storage location for transactions awaiting the completion of loading of the compiler program. Once this has been completed, the loader will place all transaction words in the list COML into the availability queue, from which point they will execute the (reentrant) compiler program. Once the current worker transaction for compiler execution has been placed in the list COML, transfer is made to connector 2 in the second chart of Fig. 21 at which point the director's remaining operations are to ascertain whether or not it is to continue its activities relative to further transactions appearing in DIRQ.

We consider now the case where the job request transaction, *T,* represents a call for a card-to-device operation. In this case, at box 3 the determination by the director causes transfer to execution of the functions of box 22. Here the available transaction, *T,* is placed onto a card-to-device queue, CTDQ. It is from this queue of transaction words that the card-to-device program selects the transactions of current interest to this operation. It should be noted here that this program is made to operate as a sequentially reusable function for the simple reason that only one device, card reader number 2, is available for the card-to-device operation.

With the job request transaction, *T,* placed onto CTDQ, the director no longer has an available transaction, as indicated by the transaction term on exit from box 22. It now goes on to execute box 23. Here the director tests whether or not the card-to-device program is core resident and available for execution. This is accomplished by the indicated interrogation of the symbolic location C1. Since this program has no need to be reentrant and therefore may be associated with its own transaction, it is stored in location C1 when the program is inactive. Hence, if the director finds C1 to be nonempty, the transfer is to box 24 where the transaction word, *C*, for this program is retrieved from the location C1, and that location is reset to zero. The transaction, *C*, now appears as the available transaction and the director transfers to connector 3 of the second chart of Fig. 21. This is an entrance to box 6 with *C* as the available transaction. The director places it onto the loader queue and thus inaugurates the loading of the card-to-device program.

In the event that the card-to-device program is already active and therefore core resident, the director transfers from box 23 to connector 2 of the second chart of Fig. 21, where its further actions involve the determination as to whether the director itself should continue relative to other transactions in its DIRQ or terminate. That is all that is required since the card-to-device program is already core resident and active, and the job request transaction, *T*, seeking its services, has been placed onto its CTDQ.

The Loader

As with the receiver and director programs, the loader will operate as an independent and asynchronous function of the operating system. Its interface with the other elements of the operating system, and most particularly with the director, is via a loader queue, or LDRQ.

The loader is the point at which memory allocation for a program is made. In order to establish a criteria for the selection of the next transaction representing the program to be loaded, let us assume that the compiler program is large relative to other programs that are generally run by the system. Since the compilation frequency is relatively high in this hypothetical system, it is desirable that the criteria for memory allocation be such as to guarantee a preferential consideration for loading of the compiler when that operation is required. Under the assumption that the compiler program itself is relatively large, in order to give it preferential consideration for loading it should be sufficient to adopt memory size as the criteria for the loader's selection of a transaction from LDRQ. Hence, when made active the loader will select a transaction word from LDRQ such that the memory space required by the program represented by this transaction word is the largest among those seeking the loader's attention. Furthermore, it is specifically assumed that allocation for this top transaction in the queue must be accomplished before loading for any other transaction may be initiated. This means that if allocation cannot be accomplished for the largest memory requirement, then no further allocations, and hence memory loading, are attempted until this largest requirement is satisfied, even though the available memory space may be sufficient to accomodate the needs of other programs represented in LDRQ. With this criteria established for the allocation of memory space, we go on to describe the loader functions as shown in the transaction chart of Fig. 22.

When the loader is activated by MPX, its transaction, *L*, is placed onto the availability queue, from which point it is ultimately selected as the current operating transaction by the multiprogram executive. When this occurs, execution of the loader function begins at connector 1 of Fig. 22.

The first operation of the loader is to select a transaction word from LDRQ. As mentioned above, this is done on the basis of the program having the largest memory requirement. Each transaction thus selected becomes the available transaction, with its transaction word placed into the AT location of the CPU item. With the transaction thus selected represented by the generic symbol *W*, its presence in the AT location of the CPU item is indicated in the CPU term on exit from box 1, which also indicates that the transaction, *L*, the loader transaction, is the COT.

It is with the transaction, *W*, that box 2 is entered. Here a call is made on the allocator program where the memory requirements for *W* are compared against the available memory. Assume that the allocator is able to allocate memory to the transaction *W*, so that the next function accomplished by the loader is that indicated in box 3. Here, the allocation of memory space is carried out, and at box 4 the actual loading of the program represented by the transaction word in the AT location is initiated. This is physically accomplished as a sequence of input operations by the loader, moving the required program in segments from the disk library. The sequence of input operations by

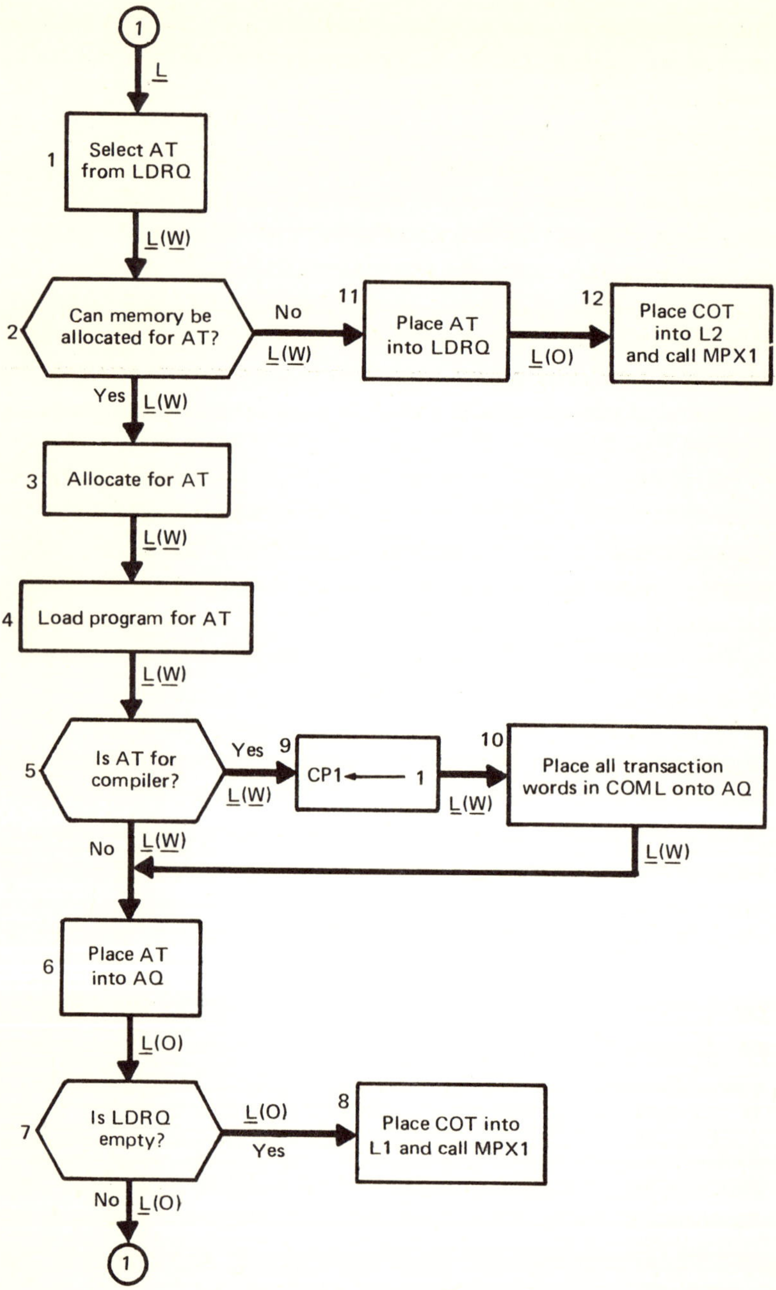
1
L
1 Select AT from LDRQ
L(W)
2 Can memory be allocated for AT?
No
L(W)
11 Place AT into LDRQ
L(O)
12 Place COT into L2 and call MPX1
Yes
L(W)
3 Allocate for AT
L(W)
4 Load program for AT
L(W)
5 Is AT for compiler?
Yes
L(W)
9 CP1 ← 1
L(W)
10 Place all transaction words in COML onto AQ
L(W)
No
L(W)
6 Place AT into AQ
L(O)
7 Is LDRQ empty?
L(O)
Yes
8 Place COT into L1 and call MPX1
No
L(O)
1

Fig. 22. LDR

the loader function is of course treated as a multiprogrammed operation, so that the loader transaction, *L*, is transferred to MPX and the I/O package treated like any other transaction, and in the handling of its input requests.

After the specified program has been loaded, the transaction *W* remains as the available transaction. With the transaction term as shown on exit from box 4, the next function executed is at box 5. Here the loader ascertains whether or not the program loaded was the compiler program. If it was not the compiler, then transfer is made to box 6 where the available transaction, *W*, is placed onto the availability queue, since the program for *W* is now in the memory in allocated locations and is indeed available for execution.

On exit from box 6, the transaction term shows that there is no longer an available transaction, since *W* has been placed onto the availability queue. Transfer is then made to box 7, where LDRQ is tested to determine if there are additional transactions requesting the loader's attention. If the queue is not empty, return is made to connector 1 to repeat the above described operations. On the other hand, if the queue is empty, then there is no further requirement for the loader at this time and hence, at box 8, the loader function places its transaction word *L* (located in the COT word of the CPU item) into the symbolic location L1, indicating to the director that the loader is inactive. The last operation in the loader at this point is to call on MPX to terminate its current activities.

Returning now to box 5, suppose that the loader determines, by interrogation of the AT, that the program for which loading has just been completed was indeed the compiler. Transfer is therefore made to box 9. At this point, the switch CP1 is set to 1 to indicate to the director function that the compiler program is now in memory. The next operation is at box 10 where all transaction words in the list COML are placed onto the AQ. These transaction words represent job request transactions for the execution of the compiler, each of which arrived subsequent to the transaction *W*, which has just caused the loading of the compiler program. With this accomplished, the loader transfers to box 6 to continue its closing operations as earlier described.

The foregoing discussion was based on the assumption that

memory was available for allocation to the transaction *W*. Returning to box 2, assume now that in handling that transaction in LDRQ with the largest memory requirement, it was found that insufficient memory was available. Hence, transfer from box 2 is made to box 11, with the transaction term as shown. The AT is still the transaction *W* and this is placed back onto the LDRQ where it will be later considered by the loader. Note now that, upon exit from box 11, the available transaction location of the CPU item is empty.

At box 12, then, the loader places the contents of the COT location, i.e. its own transaction *L*, into the symbolic location L2, and calls on MPX. The purpose of this operation is to put the loader transaction into a position where, on investigation by MPX, it can be ascertained if the loader is active but awaiting a program termination. When a termination next occurs, the consequent deallocation of assigned memory will augment the currently available space and will allow the loader to attempt the loading of that worker transaction which could not be accommodated at this time. Note in particular that the presence of the loader's transaction word in location L2 means that it is not present in the location L1, and therefore the loader is active so far as the director is concerned.

It should also be pointed out that by returning the worker transaction, *W*, to the loader queue, the opportunity exists for another transaction, *W*1, with a larger memory requirement than *W*, to appear in the loader queue and hence get prior treatment by the loader when more memory space becomes available. This is clearly in accord with the criteria established for the loading order of programs.

The Terminator

Each worker program executed by the system will transfer to MPX on termination. The function within MPX that handles termination will be referred to as the terminator, and carries out the necessary operations to deallocate devices and memory assigned to the terminating transaction, and to initiate the production of any presentation output that was developed by the transaction during its execution.

The method adopted for use of the two on-line printers is to have the worker transaction with an output destined for the printer call MPX. The I/O package, in concert with the distributor, will organize this output into printer buffers on the external random access storage. Production of this output will then be initiated at the time of termination of the worker program.

Since the terminator is responsible for the deallocation of assigned devices, it will determine if there are any transaction words for worker programs in the director list, DIRL, awaiting the availability of devices before they can be treated further by the director function. Hence, the terminator must determine if the release of devices makes worker transactions available for further processing by the director, and in the affirmative case, must move all such transactions from the director list, DIRL, back into the director queue, DIRQ.

A final function of the terminator is to ascertain whether or not the loader was previously deferred from further execution because of the lack of memory for allocation. Since the current terminating transaction releases memory in the terminator routine, this test is best carried out by this function.

The various operations of the terminator routine are shown in the transaction chart of Fig. 23. The worker transaction *W*, in executing its termination statement, transfers to MPX and arrives at connector 1 of this chart. The first function in this routine is executed by the worker transaction itself, and, as indicated at box 1, causes it to write a file sentinel in order to terminate its presentation output. This of course assumes that presentation output was prepared by *W* during its execution and hence, box 1 includes a test to this effect. It should be pointed out that this test can be accomplished merely by checking a "presentation bit," in the transaction item for *W*, which is set by the distributor program should *W* call on it at any point in its execution in order to deliver a presentation output to the printer buffer system.

The operations of box 1 are charged to the worker transaction, *W*. With this completed, it enters the O/S function of box 2, thereby crossing the entry boundary of the operating system. As described in Chapter 5, this makes the operating system trans-

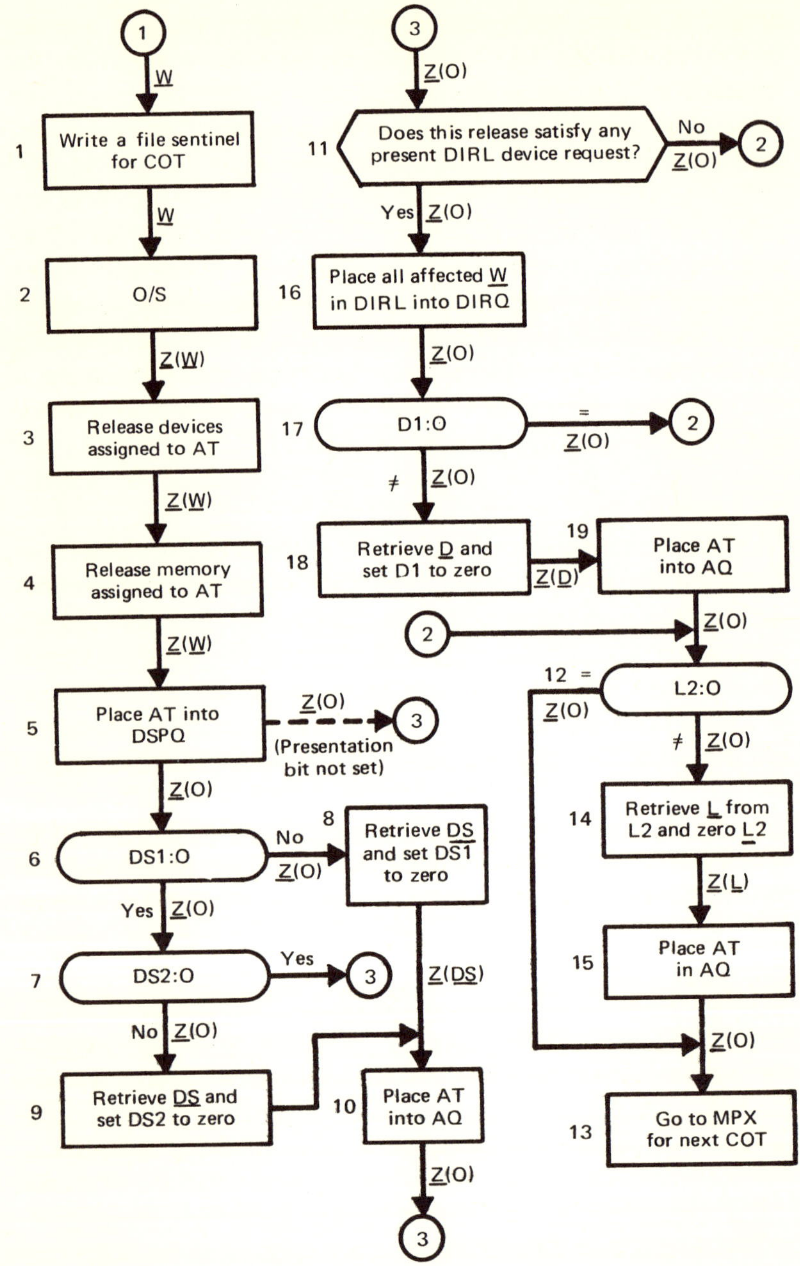

Fig. 23. Terminator

action, Z, the current operating transaction, placing its transaction word into the COT location of the CPU item. Also, the transaction word W is transferred to the available transaction location of the CPU item, and finally, in this box, the interrupts are disabled.

The transaction term on exit from box 2 is as shown in the chart, and indicates that Z is the current operating transaction with the terminating worker transaction, W, as the transaction of current interest to Z. Hence, on entrance to box 3 with W as the available transaction, devices assigned to W are released. At box 4 the memory assigned to the available transaction is released, and at box 5 the transaction word is placed into the dispatcher queue, DSPQ, for handling by the program. Of course, if at box 5 it is determined that the worker transaction did not produce output destined for the printers during its execution, then a transfer to connector 3 (box 11) is made directly.

Assuming that the worker transaction has produced output for the printer, its transaction word has been placed into DSPQ, so that on entry to box 6 the CPU term is Z (O) as indicated in the chart. At box 6, since there is at least one transaction in DSPQ at this point, the terminator must ascertain whether or not the dispatcher function is busy. In the context of the present system, "busy" means that each of the two dispatcher transactions (one for each printer) is currently present in the multiprogram set. Therefore, if the dispatcher is busy, the terminator will not discover a transaction word in either location DS1 or DS2, where the dispatcher transaction words are retained if not active. Hence, at box 6 the symbolic location DS1 is tested for the presence of the first dispatcher transaction word, and at box 7, if this transaction word is not present, the terminator tests to determine if the second dispatcher transaction word is present in DS2. If not present at this point, the CPU term remains Z (O) with a transfer made directly to connector 3 for entry to box 11, since the dispatcher is currently active and the terminating worker transaction is already in the dispatcher queue.

If either DS1 or DS2 is nonzero, at least one of the dispatcher transaction words are available so that transfer is made to either box 8 or box 9, depending on which of these words can be selected. The dispatcher transaction for one or the other of the printers is retrieved so that on entry to box 10 the CPU term is *Z* (DS), as shown.

Box 10 places the selected dispatcher transaction (now the AT) into the availability queue, from which point it will be selected by MPX for execution (possibly reentrant) of the dispatcher program. On exit from box 10, therefore, there is no longer an available transaction and hence the CPU term is as shown. The exit from box 10 is a transfer to connector 3 for entrance to box 11.

At this point, memory and devices that were assigned to the terminating transaction, *W*, have been returned to the system, and the worker transaction has been placed into the dispatcher queue. In addition, the dispatcher program has been activated if not fully active, i.e. if at least one of its transaction words is not presently in the multiprogrammed set. Hence, the next determinations of the terminator are relative to prior actions that have been taken by the director and the loader functions, so that in box 11, the terminator program asks if the release of peripheral devices (at box 3) by the terminating worker transaction satisfies any present requirements by job request transactions in the director list (DIRL) that would allow those transactions to continue their processing by the director program. Assume that the devices released by the terminating worker transaction do not satisfy the present device requirements for any transaction in the director list, so that transfer is made by the current operating transaction, *Z,* to box 12.

At box 12, the terminator program tests the symbolic location L2, which holds the loader transaction, *L,* whenever that transaction has been deferred from further execution due to a failure to allocate. Should this test show that no further action with respect to the loader need be taken by the terminator, transfer is made to box 13, which is to that portion of the multiprogram executive where a new current operating transaction will be selected.

On the other hand, if it is determined by interrogation of the symbolic location L2 that the loader transaction, *L,* is indeed present and therefore has been previously deferred from further execution, transfer is made to box 14. Here the loader transaction word is retrieved from the location L2, and that location is set to zero. On exit from box 14, therefore, the transaction term shows that *L* is the available transaction.

In box 15, then, the available transaction is placed into the availability queue, which in this case makes the loader available for further execution. In continuing its execution, the loader will retrieve that worker transaction word from the loader queue which currently has the largest core memory requirement and again attempt to allocate memory space. Hence, on exit from box 15, the CPU term shows that the AT location is empty, and transfer is made by the current operating transaction, *Z* (the operating system transaction), to box 13 for a subsequent transfer to that portion of MPX which selects a next current operating transaction.

Returning to box 11, suppose that the release of devices by the terminating worker transaction, *W*, has made it possible for job request transactions in DIRL to continue their processing through the director program. In this case, transfer is made by the operating system transaction, *Z*, to box 16 where all affected transaction words in DIRL are placed back into DIRQ for subsequent handling by the director. This leaves the available transaction location of the CPU item empty, as shown on exit from box 16.

At box 17, the terminator determines whether or not the director is busy by interrogating the symbolic location D1. If the director transaction, *D*, is not present in D1, then that program is active and therefore transfer is made to connector 2 where the above described actions relative to the loader are carried out.

On the other hand, if the director program is currently inactive, then the terminator routine finds location D1 nonempty and therefore transfers to box 18. At this point, the director transaction, *D*, is retrieved from location D1, and that location is set to zero, thus indicating that the director is active. On exit from box 18, the available transaction is *D*.

At box 19, the available transaction (the director transaction) is placed into the availability queue from which point it is eligible for selection by MPX as the COT. Following this, the operating system transaction, *Z*, executing the terminator routine, no longer has an available transaction. Therefore, the CPU term is correct as shown for a transfer to connector 2, where the terminator routine will investigate any requirements for servicing the loader transaction word.

The above described operations of the terminator routine within MPX accomplish the actions necessary to a terminating worker transaction insofar as device and memory assigned to that transaction have been returned to the system. If the terminating worker transaction has prepared output for the printer, the terminator routine has placed its transaction word into the dispatcher queue, activating the dispatcher program if necessary. Furthermore, any stalled job request transaction words in the director list that were seeking peripheral devices which were earlier not available are moved from DIRL back to DIRQ, if sufficient devices to warrant this transfer have been released by the terminating worker transaction. Finally, the terminator routine has activated the director as required, and has allowed the loader to resume its activity if its transaction word was stalled due to a lack of allocatable core memory space.

The Distributor

The distributor functions to organize output from worker programs that is destined for the printer into buffer space, with the storage space required on the disk. The unit of data transferred between the distributor and the buffer is the block, with each block consisting of a number of records, the size of which is equal to the width of a printed line. The number of records in a block will vary from worker program to worker program, as individually required, and it will be assumed for the sake of simplicity that the worker program itself is counting the number of lines to be printed per page. Hence, when the worker produces the last record for a page, we therefore assume that a sentinel indication is included in the output calling sequence for this record. The distributor tests for this page sentinel in each record received from a worker program, and when it appears, provides a page sentinel record for use by the dispatcher program. At this point the distributor considers the "block" to be full, and places it in the next position of the external buffer.

It is clear that some organization of data in this buffer is required on the disk that will allow for effective utilization by both the distributor and dispatcher programs. There are many approaches to this problem, each largely dependent on the operating characteristics of the disk itself. Since it is not the purpose of the present work to develop optimal approaches to data storage and retrieval on random access devices, we will say only that the organization of the buffer, and of the block within it, must be such as to allow the distributor to associate the next block from a worker program with the next logically sequential location within the buffer. The logically sequential locations of blocks in the buffer must then be available, and in a sequential order, on a per-worker-program basis to the dispatcher.

The distributor program operates asynchronously and independently of all other programs of the multiprogrammed set. Therefore, it has its own transaction word, referred to in the transaction chart of Fig. 24 as DT. When this transaction is made active, it is placed into the availability queue (by the I/O package of MPX) from which point it is selected as the COT. When it executes, it begins operations at connector 1 of Fig. 24.

The transaction words for worker programs requiring the distributor's attention are in the distributor queue, DTRQ, and are placed there asynchronously throughout the operation of the I/O package of MPX. The first function executed by the distributor is to select a worker transaction from DTRQ. This becomes the available transaction, as indicated on exit from box 1.

At box 2, the distributor sets the presentation bit in the transaction item of the available transaction. This presentation bit indicates to the terminator routine that the worker program has produced printer output during its execution. These operations do not change the state of the CPU item and therefore the CPU term remains as shown on exit from box 2.

At box 3, the distributor places the record being output by the available transaction into the output block associated with that transaction. At box 4, the distributor asks if a page sentinel notation is contained in this worker program call for output of the printer record. Assuming that the record being output by the worker at this time is not the end of the page, the distributor goes on to box 5 where the available transaction is placed into

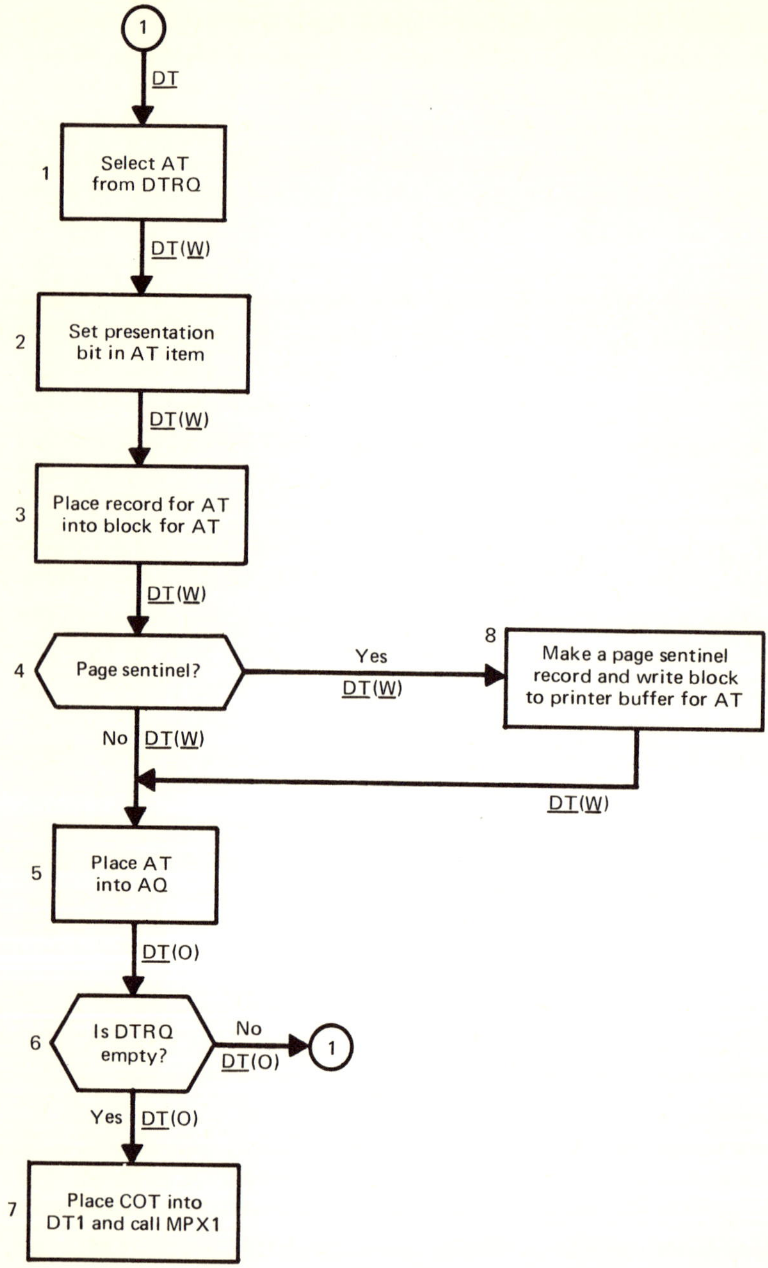
1
DT
1
Select AT from DTRQ
DT(W)
2
Set presentation bit in AT item
DT(W)
3
Place record for AT into block for AT
DT(W)
4
Page sentinel?
Yes
DT(W)
8
Make a page sentinel record and write block to printer buffer for AT
No
DT(W)
DT(W)
5
Place AT into AQ
DT(O)
6
Is DTRQ empty?
No
DT(O)
1
Yes
DT(O)
7
Place COT into DT1 and call MPX1

Fig. 24. DTR

the AQ. This makes the worker transaction available for selection at a later time by MPX, and is necessary since the current operating transaction is DT. It is in this fashion, in fact, that the distributor is able to operate asynchronously with all other members of the multiprogrammed set, and, in particular, is able to serve the multiple needs of several worker programs concurrently, as will be seen in what follows.

Since the distributor has placed the available transaction into the AQ, the AT location of the CPU item is empty, as indicated in the CPU term on exit from box 5. At box 6, DTRQ is examined to see if there are further worker transactions in that queue requiring the distributor's attention. If the queue is empty, transfer is made to box 7 where the distributor places its own transaction word DT (currently in the COT location of the CPU item) into its inactive location DT1, then calls MPX at the special location which terminates its further operation. If the distributor queue is not empty, then the transfer from box 6 is back to connector 1 to repeat the above operations for the next worker transaction word in DTRQ.

Returning to box 4, assume that the worker transaction of present interest to the distributor has specified that its current output ends a printer page. In this case, transfer is made from box 4 to box 8 where the distributor constructs a page sentinel record and writes the block of records thus far collected to the buffer associated with the AT. These operations do not change the CPU term, so that on exit from box 8 the distributor operations are continued at box 5 with *W* remaining as the available transaction.

The Dispatcher

The dispatcher program reads block of data from the printer buffers on the disk, with each record in the block to be printed as a single line on one of the on-line printers. There are two such printers in our hypothetical system, and therefore we have associated two transactions (transaction words and transaction items) with the dispatcher program, implying that this program must operate as a reentrant code. Each of these two transactions is associated with one of the printers, and as indicated earlier, is individually activated by the terminator routine of MPX at the time a worker program completes its execution.

During the execution of a worker program that has prepared output for the printer, it has made calls on the distributor (via the I/O package) which in turn has organized these records into blocks terminated by page sentinels. When the worker program terminates, the terminator routine transfers the transaction word for the worker to the dispatcher queue, DSPQ. These transaction words are placed into DSPQ asynchronously with the operation of the two dispatcher transactions, there to be picked up by these transactions as they complete one printing job and become available for the next.

The transaction chart of Fig. 25 begins its operations at connector 1, when either of the dispatcher transactions initiates its activities relative to a new printing job. This initiation is either due to activation of the selected dispatcher transaction by the terminator routine, or on completion of the last job by the dispatcher and upon discovery that further worker transaction words are present in DSPQ.

The first operation is at box 1 where the dispatcher selects a worker transaction from DSPQ and makes this the available transaction by placing it into the AT location of the CPU item. At box 2, the first block for the worker program is read from the printer buffer and printing operations are begun at box 3. The first function at box 3 is to examine the record being output by the AT to determine whether or not it is a file sentinel, i.e. if the output for the worker program is completed. This record is, of course, derived from the printer buffer block, which is currently in the memory and in the process of being transferred to the printer by the dispatcher.

In the event that the next record in the block is not a file sentinel, transfer is made to box 4 of the chart where the dispatcher examines the record to determine if it is a page sentinel. If it is not a page sentinel, then this record is output to the printer that is assigned to the particular dispatcher transaction, and return is made to connector 2 in order to accomplish the above described operations for the next record in the block associated with the AT.

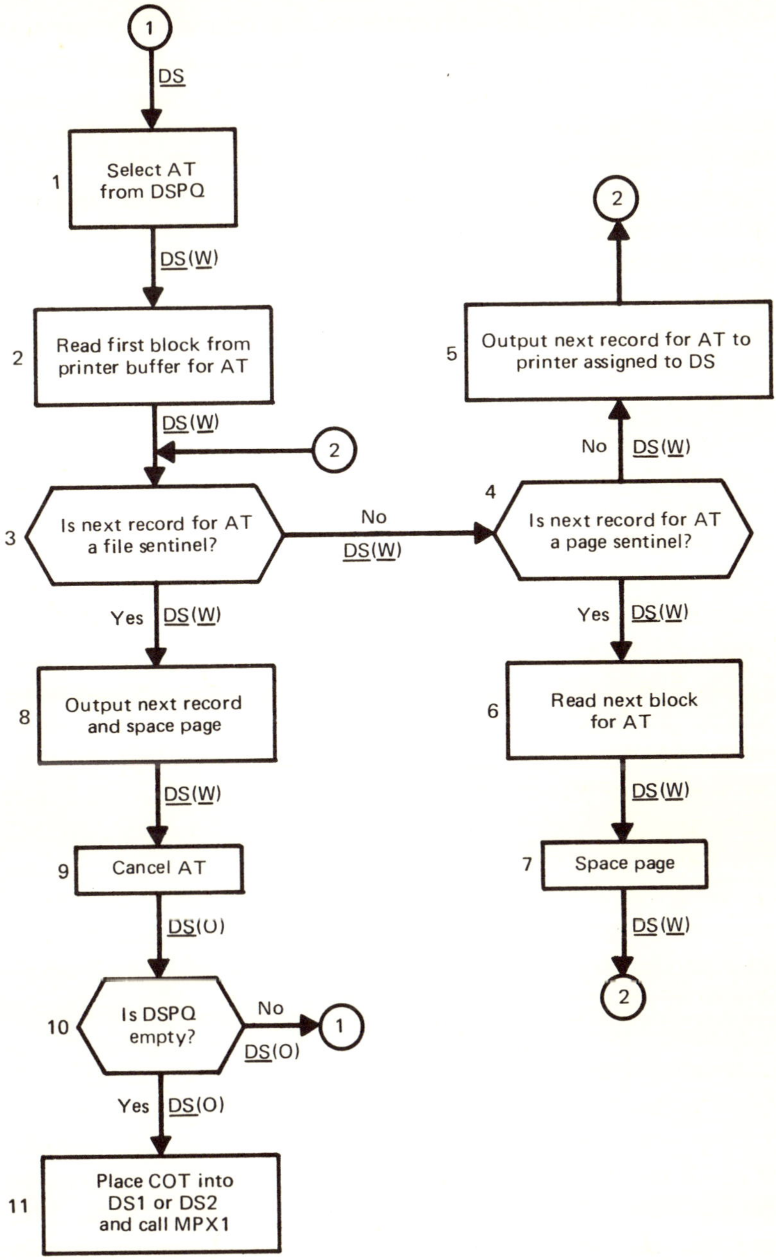
1
DS
1 Select AT from DSPQ
DS(W)
2 Read first block from printer buffer for AT
DS(W)
2
3 Is next record for AT a file sentinel?
No
DS(W)
4 Is next record for AT a page sentinel?
No
DS(W)
5 Output next record for AT to printer assigned to DS
2
Yes
DS(W)
6 Read next block for AT
DS(W)
7 Space page
DS(W)
2
Yes
DS(W)
8 Output next record and space page
DS(W)
9 Cancel AT
DS(O)
10 Is DSPQ empty?
No
DS(O)
1
Yes
DS(O)
11 Place COT into DS1 or DS2 and call MPX1

Fig. 25. DSP

Suppose that at box 4 the dispatcher determines that the next record for output is a page sentinel. In this case the dispatcher transfers to box 6, where the next block for the available transaction is read from the printer buffer (as a multiprogrammed input operation through the I/O package of MPX) after which, at box 7, the dispatcher spaces the page on the printer assigned to this particular dispatcher transaction. With these operations accomplished, the dispatcher returns to connector 2 to repeat the above described operations relative to the records in the new block just received from the printer buffer for its available transaction.

The printing operations, as described, are carried on until the dispatcher determines that the next record for the available transaction is a file sentinel. This designates the end of the printing job for the worker program. It will be recalled that the file sentinel record was produced by the worker program just prior to its entry to the terminator routine. At box 3, then, when the file sentinel record for the AT appears as the next record in the block to be treated by the dispatcher, a tranfer will be made to box 8 where this file sentinel record (containing an ending message to appear on the printer) is output, and the printer page is spaced. With these operations completed, all activities for the worker transaction in the AT location are complete and there are no further requirements on the operating system. Therefore, at box 9, the transaction word (and transaction item) for the AT can be discarded, thus erasing all memory of this worker program execution in the system. The closing operations of the dispatcher are to ascertain if further worker transactions remain in DSPQ, and if this is the case, then transfer is made to connector 1 where the next worker transaction is selected, and the job of printing its output is inaugurated.

As in the case of the other programs of the operating system, if there are no further entries in the DSPQ at box 10, then the dispatcher places its own transaction (in the COT location of the CPU item) into the associated storage location (either DS1 or DS2) used for retention of this transaction word when it is inactive. The final operation is then a call on the special entrance to MPX to terminate the execution of this dispatcher transaction.

CHAPTER 8

BUFFERED EXECUTIONS AND THE I/O TRANSACTION

Introduction

THE KEYSTONE FOR the developments in Chapters 4, 5, and 7 is the unbuffered execution of worker programs. Under this assumption the logic of MPX is determined independently of any of the characteristics of the files being used by the members of the multiprogrammed set. When programs are allowed to access their files through core memory buffers, however, the logic necessary for MPX is not so well determined as in the unbuffered case.

The central cause of this is timing. In the unbuffered case, an I/O reference by a worker program is the signal to MPX for the creation of an I/O activity, either as an input-output action, or as the establishment of a request for such action on a device directly responsible for the I/O actions taken by MPX. In the buffered case, however, the situation is somewhat different. Here I/O actions taken by the worker program may or may not result in I/O activity on the part of MPX, depending on the state of the buffers associated with the file being referenced. More specifically, it is necessary for MPX to ascertain, for a given input call by a worker program, if there is a data unit available in the buffer, if the delivered data unit empties the buffer, and in the latter case, if other buffers assigned to this program contain data units. This suggests that there is a selection of actions to be taken by MPX on an I/O call, and, further, that the action chosen is dependent on the current state of the buffers at the time of call, rather than on the call itself.

The first topic to be investigated in this chapter, therefore, is the structure of buffers and the nature of information available concerning their state. We then turn to operating system concepts and tools suited to the multiprogram control of buffered executions.

Sequential Files

We will consider that the basic information entity for data processing on the main frame, relative to a sequential file, is the "record." This is a collection of continguous core memory storage locations which, taken together, form a data area holding specified information. A contiguous collection of such records in the memory will be referred to as a "block," and we shall call the specified number of records the "blocking factor." A collection of blocks, not necessarily contiguous, on a peripheral device will be referred to as a file. Thus the block appears as the unit of data transferred between the worker program in core memory, and the file on its peripheral device. For simplicity of discussion it will be assumed that both record size and number of records per block are constant for a given file.

For our purposes in discussing I/O demand multiprogramming, we shall define a buffer, for a given worker program execution and particular file, as a collection of blocks. Thus, if a program is single buffered, double buffered, triple buffered, etc., for a particular file, then it has space reserved in the core memory for one, two, or three blocks of that file, respectively. The several blocks of a multiple buffering are associated with an ordinal sequence, i.e. first, second, third, etc. Thus, each block in a file has an ordinal, and hence sequential, logical position. This is what is meant by a "sequential file."

Within each block there is contained a specified number of records. These records have an ordinal sequence as well, so that all the records of the first block precede those of the second block, which precede those of the third block, and so on. Thus, for example, in a double buffering arrangement for a particular file in which the blocking factor is, say, six, the ordinal structure of the records in the core memory is as shown in Fig. 26. Suppose that the file associated with the buffers shown in this figure are for input. When the using program has emptied block one and after it has been refilled by the operating system, the first record of block one will then be the thirteenth record of the file, the second will be the fourteenth record, and so on.

Input Buffers

Input buffers are initially filled by "file opening" statements which result in $K * N$ records in the memory, where N is the blocking factor and K the number of blocks in the buffer. The worker program operates on the first, the second, the N-1st record of the first block, and then, in its next call, asks for the Nth record of the block.

If the worker program receives its input records by virtue of the operating system moving the next record from its location in the current block to a specified area available to the program from which it is then processed, we shall refer to the buffer ininvolved as a *type one* input buffer. On the other hand, if the program "receives" records by means of the operating system moving an address pointer to the beginning location of the next

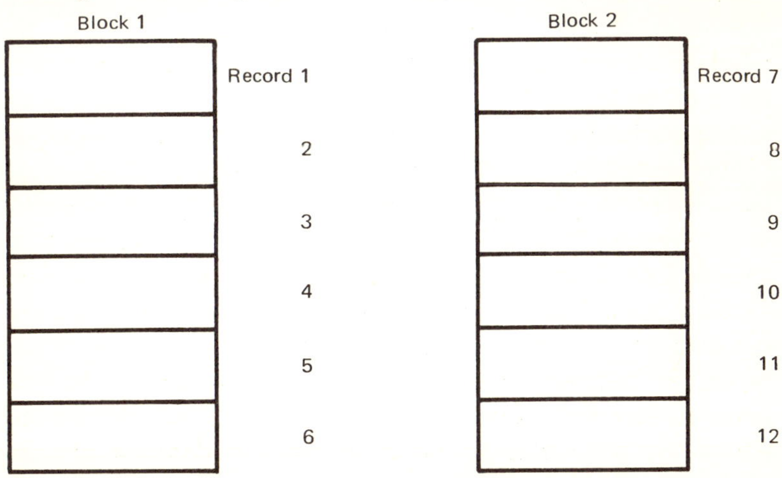

Fig. 26. Two-Block Buffer

record in the proper block, from which position processing by the program takes place, then we shall refer to this as a *type two* input buffer.

The difference between type one and type two input buffering has to do in part with capabilities of the compiler and capabilities of the addressing structure of the computer system itself. In the case of type one input buffering, the next record called for by the worker program is moved to specified locations available to that program, with the compiler providing direct access to the symbolic data subunits within this specified area. Thus the program processes data in "standard" locations and its operands reference this data directly, as opposed to indirect addressing. On the other hand, type two input buffering does not move the record but rather moves a pointer which then acts as a base address for that record. This pointer is available to the worker program so that references to the current record are made, via the pointer, as indirect addresses. This obviously requires an indirect addressing capability in the computer itself and recognition of the requirement for this type of addressing by the compiler.

Output Buffers

The operation of an output buffer is in most respects identical with the operation of an input buffer. The type one output buffer receives a record from the worker program by means of physical movement of the data involved from an area specified by the program to the next available position in the current output block of the buffer. This again is a case where the compiler has provided direct referencing in the program to the symbolic locations within the specified or "standard" area associated with the worker program. On the other hand, the type two output buffer "receives" the next record by direct emplacement of the data as it is developed by the program, with the current block location of the buffer established by means of the operating system's adjustment of an associated pointer. As in the case of type two input buffering, this means that all references by the program to this new output record location are indirect address references, and this is accomplished by a conjunction of computer and compiler activities.

Type One I/O

Consider a worker program execution that refers to a type one input buffer for one of its files. In order to initiate use of these buffers for data input by the execution of the program, it is necessary that a "file opening" statement be accomplished. This causes the transfer of blocks from the peripheral device holding the file to the core memory in sufficient numbers to fill the entire buffer for this file. On a subsequent input call from the worker program for this file, the operating system delivers the next record to the specified area. If this does not exhaust the records in the particular buffer block, then the worker program can be continued as current operating program without further delay. However, if the delivered record empties the current block, the operating system should initiate an input activity to refill this block before control is returned to the worker program. Thus, the worker program is allowed to continue operating on the last record that it has just received from this block while an input activity to refill the block proceeds in parallel. When processing of the record is completed by the program, it will return to the operating system for its next record, which is the first record of its next block in sequence in the buffer.

After the last record of its last buffer block has been received by the worker program, and an input operation has been initiated to refill that block, the program may return for its next record. In this case, it receives the first record in the first block in the buffer.

It is clear that at some point during the processing of records, causing a cycle of inputs to each block of the buffer in their specified sequence, the worker program may seek a record from the next block before that block has been refilled by the input operation initiated earlier when its last record was removed. When this occurs, it is assumed that the current operating program cannot continue until this next record becomes available, and here it is multiprogrammed, i.e. its further execution is deferred, and a new current operating program is selected. Thus, if there is a temporary delay due to lack of data in one file, the worker program is not provided the option of continuing on an alternate processing route. This approach has a number of advantages, the most significant of which is that multiprogramming control is up to the operating system entirely, rather than at the whim of the programmer and his willingness to use "relinquish" instructions.

The operation of a type one output buffer is in most respects identical to the operation of a type one input buffer. The worker program enters the operating system with the next record for output. This record is physically moved from a location standard with respect to the worker program into the next available record location within the buffer block currently being filled. When the last record for the block has been placed, the operating system initiates an output activity from that block and returns to the worker program. The next record with which the program enters for output is then emplaced as the first record in the next block of the buffer.

As in the case of the input buffer, it is possible that the worker program seeks to emplace a record before output from the next block in the buffer block sequence has been completed. In this case, the worker program will be multiprogrammed, and a new current operating program will be selected.

In order to get the last block written from the memory to the associated file, the worker program must execute a "file closing" statement. This will cause the operating system to pad out the current block and to place a sentinel record after the last record in the block. It will also initiate output of this last block to the associated file.

Type Two I/O

The above description of type one input and output buffering is distinguished by the fact that the record to be input to, or output from, the worker program is physically positioned relative to a location that is standard with respect to the program. This is accomplished either before processing, in the case of an input record, or after processing is completed, in the case of an output record. It is because of this, therefore, that an input operation is initiated immediately after the last record has been removed from a buffer block, and an output operation is initiated immediately after the last record has been emplaced in a buffer block.

For type two buffering, an input operation is not initiated until the program seeks access to the first record in its next block. When this occurs it is assumed that no further operations will be carried out on the last record of the previous block, and therefore the operating system at this time can initiate an input to that block. This means that there is no need to physically transfer the record to a standard location, and as a consequence the worker program may process that record in place. The problem for the operating system in designating the next record for input to the program merely involves varying a base address register or location, which then becomes the origin for operations by the worker program with respect to the current record of this particular file.

In a similar fashion for type two output buffers, the last block that has been filed cannot be written until the worker program returns to the operating system to "emplace" what will then be the first record of the next block. When this occurs, the operating system may assume that all processing on the last record of the previous block is completed and therefore can initiate an output operation to the associated file. As in the previous case, the record is not physically moved, but rather is processed into the output record location. More specifically, this means that the next output record can be constructed in the current output block locations.

The file opening and closing statements required for type one buffering are used for the same purposes in type two buffering. The conditions for multiprogramming of worker programs, however, are somewhat different in this second case. After a worker program has completed processing on the last record of a type two output buffer, it must enter the operating system to advance its output record reference to the first record position of its next output block. If at this time the operating system determines that the output initiated earlier for this next block is not yet complete, then further execution of the worker program is deferred, and a new COT is selected. In the case of an input buffer of this type, the worker program returns to the operating system for the location of its next input record. If this new reference is to the first record of its next block, but a previously initiated input to that block has yet to be completed at this time, then the worker is multiprogrammed and, as before, a new current operating program selected.

Thus, as in the case for type one buffering, the worker program is not allowed an alternative path in the event that the rate of processing with respect to one of the files being used exceeds the rate at which either new data can be input, or processed data can be output.

Some General Remarks

Type two buffering is most efficient when the program is able to operate from the data contained in the input records directly into the production of output records. In this case, the system saves the superfluous physical transfer of records into and out of their respective buffers relative to the "standard" locations of type one buffering. Against this is an inherent I/O inefficiency associated with type two buffering. This derives from the fact that I/O activity relative to the last buffer block used cannot be initiated until the next record reference to that file is made by the worker program. That is, the operating system cannot inaugurate an input/output activity relative to the current block until it is certain that activity relative to the last record in that block is complete. The signal for this is access to the next record of the file by the worker program, i.e. reference to the first record of the next block in the buffer block sequence. This means therefore, that for type two buffering, I/O activity is not initiated until all processing has been completed with respect to the current buffer block, whereas in type one buffering I/O activity can be initiated at the time of reference to the last record of the current block and may proceed in parallel with the processing of this last record.

In summary then, type one buffering requires physical movement of records in the core memory with an attendant CPU cost, and in return provides for parallel I/O activity relative to the last record of a given buffer block. In contrast to this, type two buffering offers a more efficient utilization of the CPU by virtue of direct computations on input and output records without the need to physically move them. Against this advantage however, the type two buffering technique cannot allow for the initiation of an I/O activity until all processing relative to the current buffer block is completed, as signaled by the program's call for the next record in the file.

Thus in the type one case, there is a loss of CPU efficiency, while in the type two case there is a potential loss of utilization efficiency of peripheral equipments.

The I/O Transaction

In order to properly discuss operating systems that allow worker programs to execute with type one or type two buffers, it is convenient to introduce the notion of the I/O transaction. The purpose of the I/O transaction is to represent a particular input or output activity generated by the execution of a worker program. That is, when the worker program executes an I/O statement, it creates an I/O transaction that is then used to represent the designated I/O activity. This is in many respects similar to the CPU transaction introduced earlier, and consists of a transaction item plus a transaction word, where the content of the transaction word is the address of the transaction item. As for the I/O transaction item, it contains information necessary to the operating system's correct handling of the specific I/O reference made by the worker program.

A point of major interest here is that a given worker program refers to certain files. A specific execution (possibly reentrant) of this program will therefore be associated with a specific set of buffers in the core memory, one for each of these files. In this sense then, all data pertaining to the state of the buffers for a particular execution, and other information necessary for linking the records of the file with the worker program, must be contained in an entity that is local to the execution of that program. This entity is the I/O transaction item. The I/O transaction word associated with the I/O transaction item serves as a convenient manipulatory unit for the operating system.

Creating I/O Transactions

One consequence of the transaction concept is to conceive of the "program" as an essentially inert element of the computing system which by its presence alone requires no more of the system than the memory space it occupies. In this sense then, the program may be thought of as a "plan" for the use of computing system resources when that program is "executed." In our conception of the operating system, we have looked upon the transaction as that entity in the system that uses resources according to the "plan" of the program that is "executed," or rather, through which the transaction "passes." From this point of view then, we might say that the execution of a program is the passing of a transaction over its instructions, during the course of which certain of these instructions will cause computations to be made, others will cause transfers of the transaction into the operating system for specified reasons, and still others will create a second kind of transaction defined above as the I/O transaction.

Thus, there are two types of transactions with which the operating system will have to deal. The first of these is the CPU transaction, already familiar from earlier discussions, which represents the particular execution of a given worker program. In order to handle such executions that refer to buffered files, it is therefore necessary to introduce the second type of transaction, known as the I/O transaction, with the understanding that these are generated by the CPU transactions according to the "plan" of the program which they are assigned to execute, i.e. when the CPU transaction passes over instructions such as READ, WRITE, PRINT, etc.

The I/O transaction conceptually plays much the same role as the CPU transaction relative to the operating system. In the case of the CPU transaction, it was represented literally by a transaction item and an associated transaction word. This allows the transaction word to be manipulated by the operating system while always retaining the identity of the transaction item with which it is associated, and through it, with the program whose execution it represents.

Similarly, the I/O transaction consists of a transaction item and a transaction word. The I/O transaction word is available for manipulation by the operating system and identifies the particular I/O transaction item with which it is associated. In subsequent discussions we will distinguish between these two types of transactions by referring to them respectively as the I/O and CPU transactions, as the situation requires. In addition, when dealing with the transaction words we shall refer to them simply as I/O and CPU words whenever the context admits a suitable clarity.

The I/O Transaction Item

Figure 27 is a schematic representation of both a CPU and an I/O transaction. In this figure, the CPU and I/O transaction items have been combined into a single information entity. The

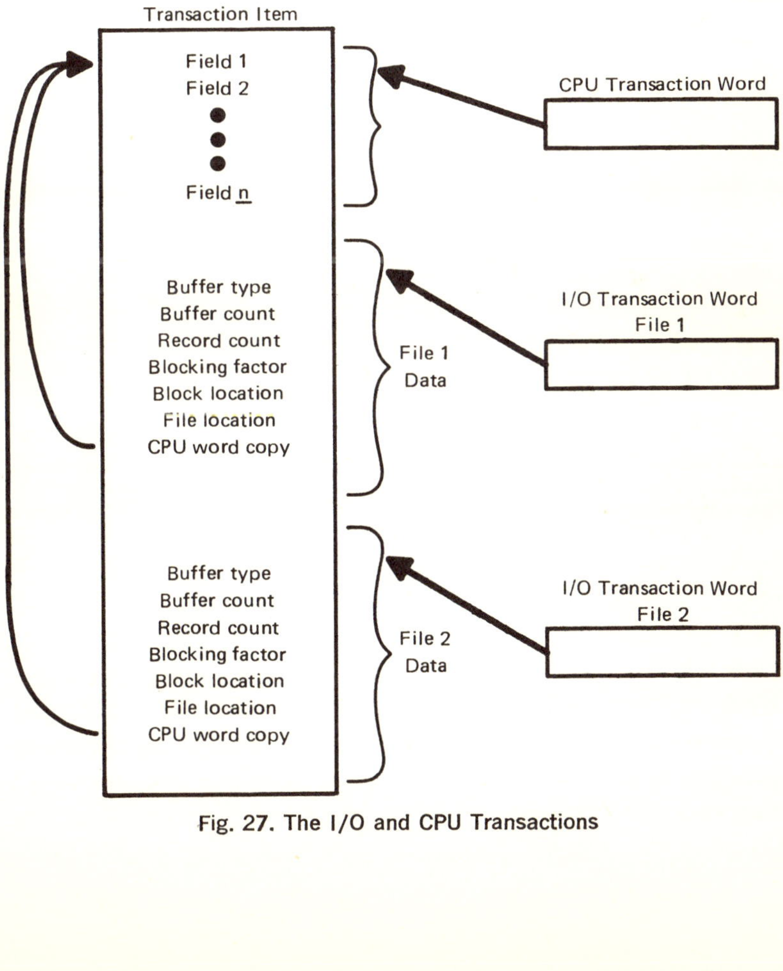

Fig. 27. The I/O and CPU Transactions

associated CPU and I/O words point to the particular portions of the transaction item with which they are concerned. Thus in this example, the CPU transaction word identifies the location of the CPU portion of the transaction item, here shown as consisting of the first several fields. In addition, the figure shows two I/O transaction words for each of two files associated with this transaction. The first I/O word points to that portion of the transaction item containing the file information whose current activity this word is representing. Similarly, the second I/O word points to a second portion of the transaction item containing the file information with which it is associated.

It should be clear that each I/O word represents a current active requirement on the file with which it is associated through the corresponding I/O transaction item. Thus, there may be in existence at any given time several I/O words that have been generated by a given CPU transaction, each of which represents a current requirement for a record on a particular file. Furthermore, at any given moment there may be several I/O words representing a current requirement on the same file, and finally, there may, of course, be many I/O words simultaneously present for manipulation in the operating system, and which represent each of the above types of calls on the several files associated with the various CPU transactions currently resident in the system.

The I/O transaction item must contain a unit of information for each of the files that the CPU transaction might encounter in passing through the program. The unit of information required for the purposes of the operating system's control of buffering is, at a minimum, that shown in Fig. 27. In this figure, "buffer type" is a coding which specifies whether the buffer is for input or output, and of type one or type two. The "buffer count" is initially the total number of blocks to be associated with this file for this execution of the given program. When an input buffer block is emptied by the program, the buffer count is reduced by unity. When that buffer block is refilled, the count is increased by unity. Similarly, when an output buffer block has been filled by a program, this count is reduced by unity, and increased by unity when the data the block contains has been transferred to the peripheral device on which its file resides. Thus, the buffer count is used to indicate the number of blocks currently available for use by the worker program, including the block whose records are currently being processed. Because the buffer control described in the next section is transaction dependent, the number of buffer blocks associated with each independent (possibly concurrent) execution of a given program may be different. The "record count" applies to the current input buffer block and specifies the number of records still remaining in it to be processed, or delivered, to the program. For an output buffer, it represents the number of record positions remaining before the current block is filled. The "blocking factor" is, as defined earlier, the number of records per buffer block. It is used by the operating system to restore the record count. The "block location" is the memory address of the first record position of the first buffer block assigned for this execution. It is assumed that the remaining blocks in the buffer are either physically contiguous in the memory or are logically contiguous by means of address linking in the buffer itself or by listing all of the buffer block locations in the I/O transaction item for this file. The "file location" is sufficient information for locating the represented file on its peripheral device.

The purpose of the I/O transaction is to provide an object suitable for representing I/O activity in the system that proceeds in parallel with the parent CPU transaction. This implies that I/O transactions will have to synchronize with their respective CPU transactions, and "CPU word copy" provides one general approach to its accomplishment.

The I/O transaction item is constructed at the same time as the CPU transaction item. This occurs when the call for program execution is entered in the system and after sufficient information has been garnered from the job request (by the director) to allow for construction of the I/O transaction item. Hence, the I/O transaction item for a given file is associated with a specific execution of some program and, more particularly, with a specified number of buffer blocks for that execution. The I/O transaction words, however, are not created at this time but rather dynamically as the CPU transaction encounters the I/O statements of the program through which it passes. Thus, each execution of an I/O statement by a CPU transaction creates a corresponding transaction word. The content of this transaction word is the address of the information in the I/O transaction item designated for the file specified by the I/O statement in the program.

Extension of the CPU Item

The CPU item was earlier defined as a two-word item located in fixed addresses in the core memory that are available to the operating system. The first word of the CPU item is designated as the current operating transaction, or COT location, and holds the name, i.e. transaction item address, of the CPU word to which the CPU is currently assigned. The second word of the CPU item is for the available transaction (AT) and is used by the operating system when it is COT to aid in its manipulation of other transactions in the multiprogram set. In order to introduce a capability for the manipulation of I/O transactions, the CPU item is extended to include a third word that will be used to hold an I/O transaction word of current interest to the operating system. This will be designated as the IOT location of the CPU item.

As an example of the application of the IOT location of the CPU item, consider the case where a worker program transaction, *W*, acting as COT, executes a READ statement in its program. This creates, in the first place, a specific I/O transaction word, the content of which is the address of the information for the designated file in the I/O transaction item. This word will be designated as *w*. The second action taken by the transaction *W* is to transfer to the operating system, crossing an operating system boundary via the O/S function as earlier described. The effect of the entry into the operating system is to make the operating system transaction, *Z*, the current operating transaction, and to make the worker transaction, *W*, the available transaction. Hence, on crossing the operating system entrance boundary, the CPU item has in its COT location the operating system transaction word, *Z*, in its AT location the worker program transaction word, *W*, and in its IOT location the generated I/O transaction word, *w*. These last two transaction words are now available for manipulation by the current operating transaction, *Z*. Figure 28 is a summary of these actions that generate the I/O transaction word in the IOT location of the CPU item.

In the following sections, we discuss the "buffer" function in detail. The purpose of this function is to ascertain the current state of a specified I/O buffer, carrying out the required operations relative to the given file information. The file information of interest at the time of execution of the buffer function is one designated by the I/O transaction word currently located in the IOT position of the CPU item. In Chapter 9 the modification of the CPU term for transaction chart respresentation of the CPU item will be discussed.

Type One Input Buffer States

Throughout our discussions, we shall refer to a certain programming to be known as the "buffer" function. The purpose of this function is to determine the input/output state of the buffer specified by a given I/O transaction, designating the alternatives to be taken.

For each type of buffer thus far considered and for which we seek to develop a control technique, there exists three distinct I/O states. Consider first the case for type one input buffering. In this instance, if the program is about to receive an input record that is not the last record in the current buffer block, then we shall say that it is in the *A* state. If the program is about to receive the last record in its current buffer block, we shall say it is in its *B* state. If the program seeks the first record from its next buffer block, but refilling of that block has yet to be completed, then we shall say it is in its *C* state. Virtually identical states can be identified for type one output buffers and for the type two buffers.

Since reference to any I/O activity by a program, as executed by its associated CPU transaction, becomes the responsibility of the operating system, it is necessary to provide the operating system with a function capable of determining for a specific I/O transaction precisely the state of the buffers to which the CPU

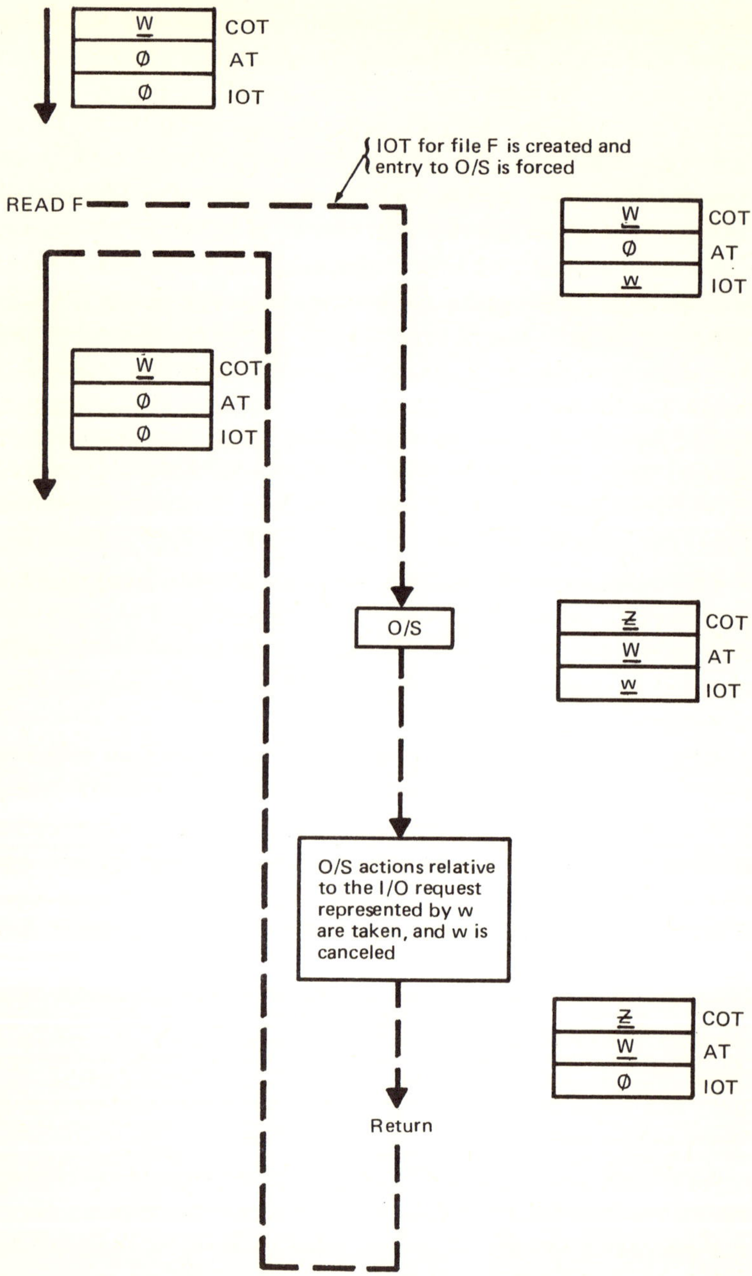

Fig. 28. Application of the IOT Location

transaction is assigned. This is the buffer function mentioned earlier.

The Type One Input Buffer

We consider now the logical operations that the type one input buffer function must carry out in order to determine the current state of the input buffer associated with a given I/O transaction. We take as the specified transaction that one indicated by the I/O word found in the IOT location of the CPU item. This will be referred to as the I/O transaction, *w*. Figure 29 is a flow chart presenting the logic of this buffer function.

The current operating transaction enters at box 1, where the "buffer count" field in the I/O transaction item for *w* is examined. If the buffer count is nonzero, the execution proceeds to box 2 where the "record count" field of *w* is reduced by unity and, at box 3, the next record in sequence in this buffer block is delivered, i.e. transferred to the program associated with *w*. Used in this fashion, therefore, the value at any moment of the "record count" field for a given transaction contains the number of records remaining in the current buffer block that are yet to be delivered to the program. Hence the test at box 4 determines whether or not this call delivers the last record to the particular worker program. If it does not, and there is at least one record remaining in this block, then the buffer is currently in the *A* state as defined earlier, and an exit is made from the buffer function accordingly.

Suppose on the other hand that with the delivery of the present record the buffer block is now empty. In this case, the buffer is currently in the *B* state and the indicated exit is made. However, before this exit, it is necessary to reduce by unity the count of the total number of buffer blocks available for processing (box 5), and to restore the buffer count to the value of the blocking factor. This indicates to the next execution of the buffer function for this I/O transaction, *w*, that it is to remove the first record of the next block in the buffer block sequence.

The final state of exit from the buffer function is that one in which no further information is available from the buffer specified by *w* for delivery to the calling program at this time. Re-

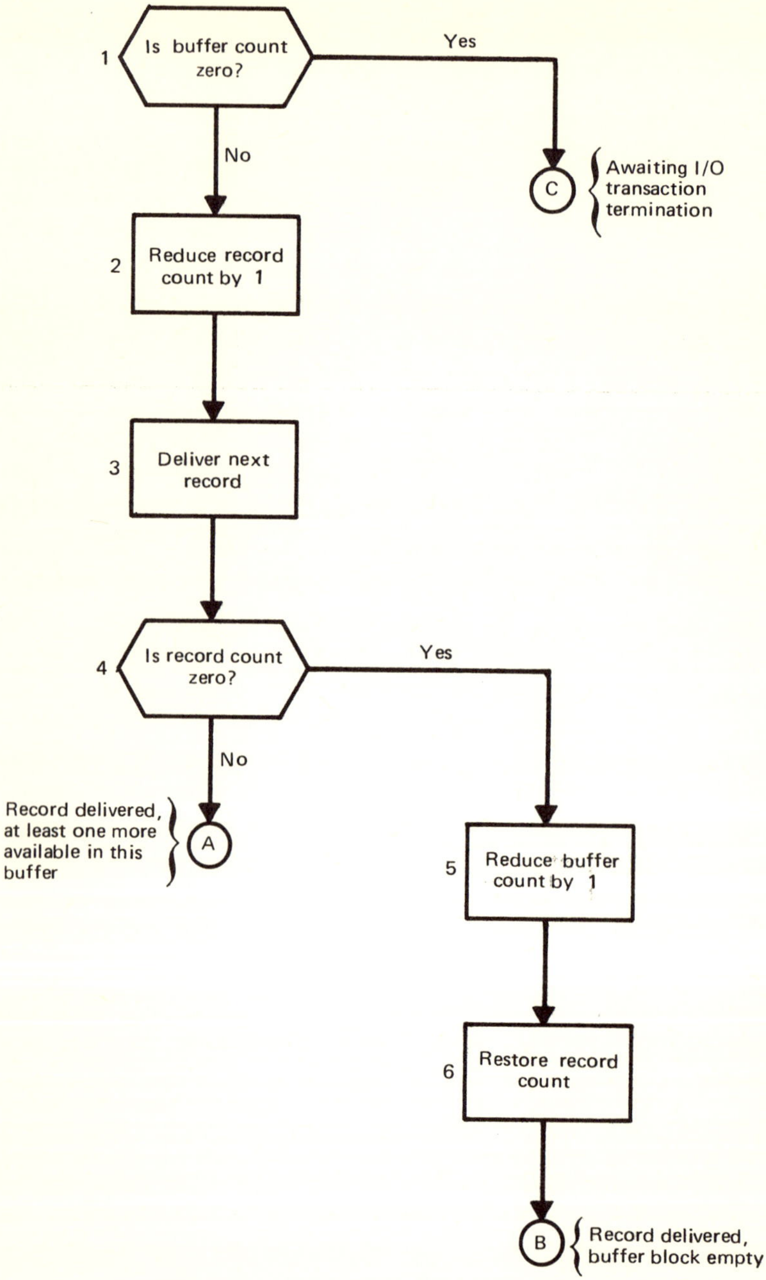

Fig. 29. The Type One Input Buffer Function

turning to the execution of box 1, this situation is reflected by the value of "buffer count" for the I/O transaction, *w,* having the value zero. This indicates that there are no records available in the next buffer block for *w,* i.e. the buffer is empty. This state is designated by an appropriate exit from the buffer function as shown.

In order to insure a complete understanding of the operation of the buffer function, the example of a two block buffering arrangement, having a blocking factor of three, is shown in Fig. 30. This is for a type one input. In this figure, starting at (*a*), the three records in each of the two blocks are shown, along with the current contents of the "buffer count" and "record count" fields on successive executions of the buffer function for this I/O transaction. Each of the buffer conditions shown apply when the current operating transaction is about to enter the buffer function. The indicated state is determined on exit from the buffer function.

At (*a*) no records have been delivered to the program at the time of entrance and therefore the buffer and record counts are at two and three respectively. Hence, as indicated, the buffer function will determine the state of this buffer to be *A*. In (*b*) on the second execution of the buffer function for this I/O transaction, the record count has been reduced by one, and the buffer count has remained the same. Therefore, the buffer is still in the *A* state. However, the situation changes in (*c*) since the record count has been reduced to one, indicating that for this execution of the buffer function, the last record will be removed from this block. Hence the buffer state is *B*. On the next execution of the buffer function for this I/O transaction (*d*), the buffer count will have been reduced by unity to one, and the record count restored to the blocking factor value, three. Delivery of records will now be made from the second buffer block, and if the operating system had been so structured, the I/O transaction will have caused initiation of an input operation to read a new block of data into the first of the buffer blocks. In all events, at (*d*) the next record is available for the transaction, and its delivery does not empty this buffer block. Therefore, the state that applies is *A*. Similarly in (*e*), the buffer is in the *A*

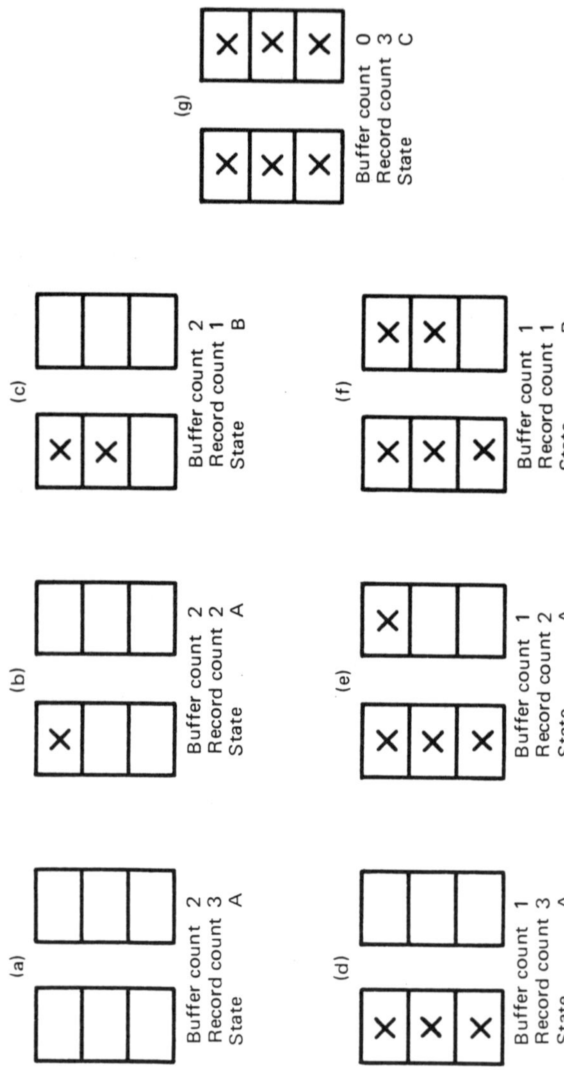

Fig. 30. Two-Block Buffer Example

state. However, at (*f*), since the record count has been reduced to one on entry to the buffer function, the last record of the second buffer block is about to be removed, and therefore the buffer is in the *B* state.

Example (*g*) now shows the situtation after the last *B* state exit from the buffer function. Here the buffer count has been reduced by unity to zero, and the record count has been restored to the blocking factor value, three. Thus, if an I/O operation to fill the first block has not been completed by the time the program returns for its next record, then the buffer count will be zero, and the buffer will be found to be in the *C* state. On the other hand, if an I/O operation earlier initiated for the first buffer block reaches a termination before the program returns for its next record, the buffer count will have been incremented and therefore will be nonzero for the next execution of the buffer function. Should this occur, the buffer will be found to be in the *A* state.

The Type One Output Buffer

Figure 31 is a flow chart giving the logic for the type one output buffer function. It is immediately apparent, by comparison with Fig. 29, that the topological structure of this flow chart is identical to that of the type one input buffer function. Furthermore, they only differ in one particular operation, namely, that one associated with box 3 where the record received from the program is emplaced in the buffer for output. Since this distinction between input and output is dependent on the definition of the buffer involved, it is part of the data carried in the I/O transaction item. Thus, these two functions may, in fact, be identical and therefore combined in a single program with the distinction as to whether a record is being delivered to, or emplaced in, the given buffer determined from the associated I/O transaction item.

The Type Two Buffer

Type two buffering, it will be remembered, allows the program to operate on records in place, rather than moving them between the buffer and some allocated storage for processing. The effect of this difference in the two types of buffering is eventually reflected in time of change of the buffer states. Thus, we shall say that the buffer is in its *A* state if, at the outset of the execution of the type two input buffer function, there is at least one record in the buffer block remaining to be treated by the program. We will say that the buffer is in its *B* state when at the

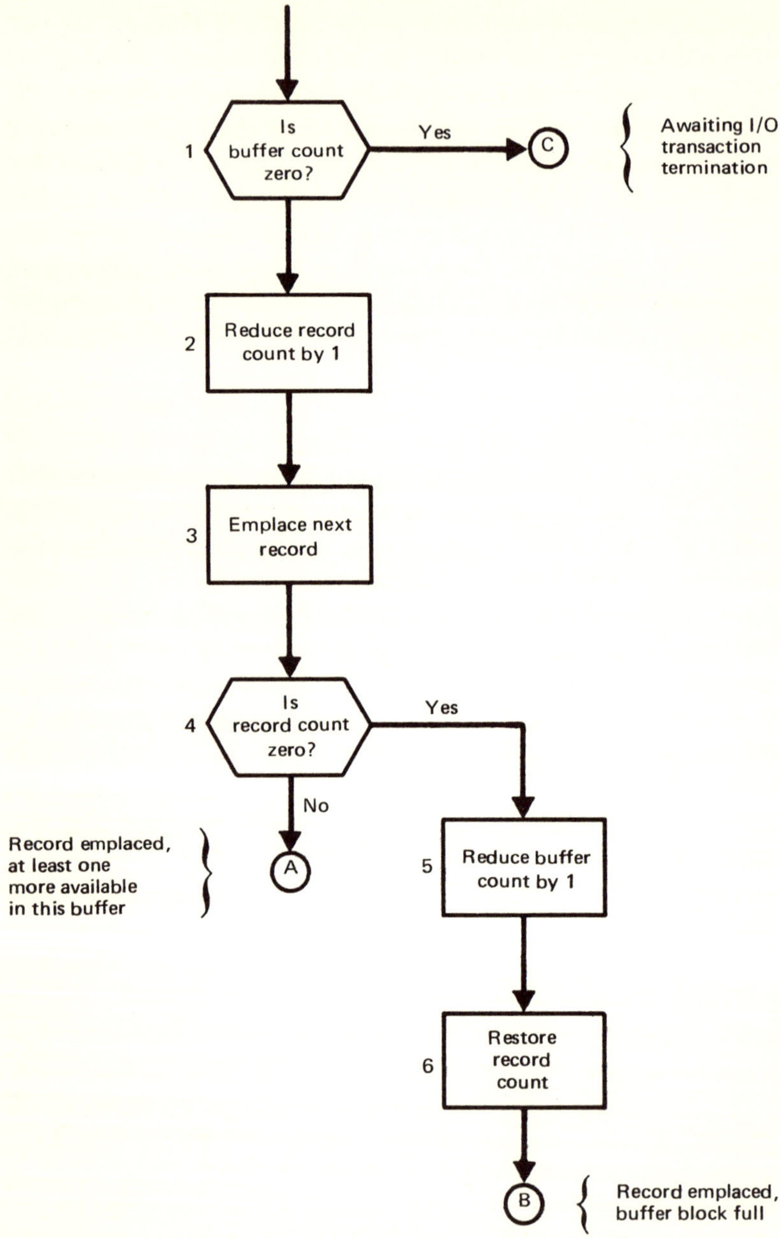

Fig. 31. The Type One Output Buffer Function

outset of the initiation of the buffer function there are no records remaining to be treated in that buffer block. Finally, we will say that the buffer is in the *C* state if, at the outset of the execution of the buffer function, the next record in the sequence is not available because it is the first record of a next buffer block, and that block has yet to be filled.

The three buffer states apply equally well to the type two output buffer, and, as will be seen, these two functions may share the same coding in their implementations. We begin with the discussion of the type two input buffer function, the flow chart for which is shown in Fig. 32.

As before, the "buffer count," "record count," and "blocking factor" fields of the I/O transaction item for the particular file will be used to determine the current buffer state and to modify and restore that state. Referring to Fig. 32, execution of the buffer function is initiated at box 1. As in our earlier discussion of type one buffering, we shall assume that the I/O transaction for which the buffer function is being executed is *w*. Thus, the first action taken is to determine if the record count for *w* is equal to zero. We will assume for the moment that it is not, so that at box 2 the value of the record address register is increased, making it refer to the next record in the buffer block. At box 3, the record count for *w* is reduced by unity, and the exit from the buffer function then indicates that the buffer was found to be in the *A* state for this I/O transaction. Thus it should be clear that the current value of the "record count" field for an I/O transaction is the number of records in the current block yet to be treated by the program.

When the value of the record address register is increased to refer to the last record in the buffer block, the next step (box 3) reduces the record count to zero. This means that on the next execution of the buffer function for *w*, the value of the record count will be zero, so that the execution of box 1 is followed by execution of box 4. Here the buffer count for *w* is reduced by unity. This implies that the current value of the "buffer count" field for the transaction originally contains the total number of blocks assigned to this buffer, and that the value of this field at any time indicates the number of these buffer

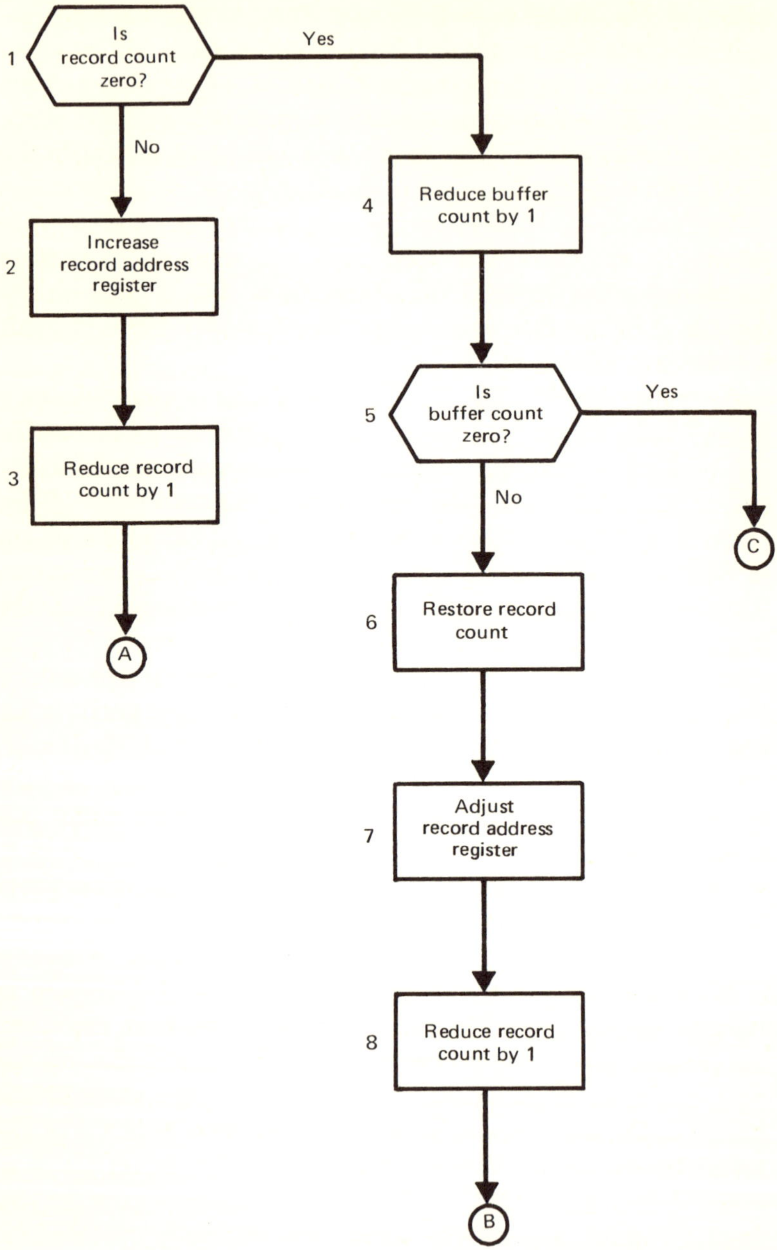

Fig. 32. The Type Two Input Buffer Function

blocks that contain records yet to be handled by the program, including the block currently supplying records. Since this is the meaning of the buffer count of the transaction *w*, the next step is to determine if this value is equal to zero. This is accomplished at box 5, and for the moment we shall assume that the value of the buffer count is nonzero. In this case the record count, previously determined to be zero at box 1, is restored (box 6).

The restoration of the record count is by means of the blocking factor for *w*. The record address register for this transaction is then adjusted so that references will be made to the first record of the next buffer block in the sequence. This is accomplished at box 7, and at box 8 the record count is reduced by one to indicate that there is one less record in the buffer block now awaiting processing by the program. Prior to these adjustments having been made then, at the outset of the execution of the buffer function under the above described conditions, the buffer is determined to be in the *B* state. The indicated exit is made to reflect this.

The final condition under which execution of the buffer function may be initiated will find the buffer concerned in its *C* state. Therefore, the last record of the last buffer block will have been handled by the program so that the record count is now at zero. On the next call for execution of the buffer function, the query at box 1 will result in a transfer to box 4, and the query at box 5 will find the buffer count equal to zero. Hence, an exit is made to indicate that the buffer is in the *C* state, as indicated in Fig. 32.

The essential difference between the type two input buffer and the type two output buffer is in the actual I/O operation associated with their respective *B* states. In the first case, an input operation is required, whereas in the second case, an output operation is required. Other than that, all operations for either delivering data from an input buffer block, or emplacing data in an output buffer block, as specified by the record address register, are the same. Therefore, the logic of the buffer function is clearly indifferent to the directional flow of data between buffer and program.

The problem of distinguishing between buffers for input, and buffers for output of this type is resolved by reference to the I/O transaction item associated with a particular type two I/O word.

Summary

This chapter has addressed itself to certain fundamental organizations necessary to the extension of the techniques thus far developed to operating systems that allow for the buffered execution of I/O by worker programs. The central criterion has been the retention of buffer control by the operating system. This criterion is derived from the general idea, expressed earlier in Chapter 3, that the current operating worker program is deferred from further execution when its current rate of operation exceeds the buffering capacity assigned to any one of its files.

With this in mind, our developments in this chapter have resulted in an extension of the CPU item concept so as to encompass I/O transactions, and thereby provide the operating system with the capability for manipulating I/O transaction words. In addition, we have developed the operating system buffer function which then becomes the basic tool in the development of an operating system capable of providing the type of buffering control under consideration. It should be noted, however, that the buffer function is merely a tool in operating system design, much as computer instructions are merely tools in the writing of programs. In this sense then, the buffer function performs specific, well defined operations and may be employed in any context that does not violate the logic specified for these operations. As such, therefore, the buffer function can be seen as a decision operator available for application in an operating system as required. The conditions for its application, however, depend upon the operating system context in which the buffer function is embedded.

CHAPTER 9

THE PROTOTYPE MPX

Introduction

IN THIS CHAPTER, we develop a "prototype" multiprogram executive for handling the buffered execution of worker programs in the multiprogram set. This MPX is a prototype in the sense that it implements the I/O demand multiprogramming requirements for buffered I/O, as discussed in Chapter 3. The major tool for this executive is the buffer function of Chapter 8, the execution of which characterizes the state of a given input/output buffer for a particular I/O transaction in terms of selecting one of the three available exits from this function. These exits describe the condition of the buffer, but only imply actions that might be taken by MPX. Thus, the prototype under discussion in the present chapter is designed to realize these implications directly. In the broader context of an executive embedded in a problem oriented operating system, containing acceptance and presentation portions, the actual structure of MPX might be quite different.

The CPU Term

We have earlier described the CPU term as that transaction chart notation which indicates, at each point of the transaction chart logic, the identity of both the current operating transaction and any current CPU transaction of interest. The CPU term took the form *A* (*B*), where *A* is the name of the current operating transaction, or COT, and *B* is the name of the available transaction, or AT. The available transaction was further described as the one of current interest to the COT at those points in the transaction chart logic where it appears in the AT position of the CPU term. Both the COT and AT were defined to be CPU transactions, and the notation for the CPU term was taken as a symbolic form of the literal representation, within the actual operating system, of the COT and AT locations of the CPU item.

In the previous chapter, the CPU item was expanded to contain an IOT location to hold an available I/O transaction word. As indicated in that chapter, the purpose of the IOT is to designate the I/O transaction word and transaction item that are of current interest to the multiprogram executive when the COT, *Z*, executes a buffer function. We therefore redefine the CPU term to include the IOT so that we may have a symbolic unit for representation of the CPU item throughout the transaction chart. The form that the CPU term will take is *A* (*B*,*c*). Where (as before) *A* and *B* are the names of CPU transactions, i.e. CPU words, and *c* is the name of the I/O transaction of current interest to the COT.

Transaction Operators

With this notational formalism established for the transaction charts, we now turn to the definition of sixteen "transaction operators" that are useful in the exposition of the logic of the buffered MPX. As will be seen, these operators have the characteristics of statements in a programming language. Their syntactic structure is generally as follows: alphabetic character string followed by a parameter enclosed in parentheses; followed by a character string; followed by a parameter, again in parentheses.

The parameters appearing in these definitions will generally consist of one or two attribute names separated by "/" implying an alternative selection. Furthermore, each of these attribute names will represent data to be found in either the CPU item, the CPU transaction item, or the I/O transaction item. The distribution of these attributes into these three categories is shown in Fig. 33. Thus, for instance, if "CPU word copy" is used as a parameter specification in one of these operators, then the reference is to the I/O transaction item and therefore that operator must be entered with an available I/O word in the IOT of the CPU item.

The purpose of this formalism is not to be exhaustive and exacting in terms of a compiler language, but rather to excise, as much as possible, the potential for ambiguity in the transaction charts. Since the problem of MPX is generally the manipulation of CPU and I/O words, it will be seen that these statements are sufficient to provide an explicit and formal (if not in each detail exacting) presentation of the necessary logical operations.

Buffer (One/Two)

This operator is entered with an I/O word in the IOT location of the CPU item. By reference to the I/O transaction item that is indicated by the I/O word, the buffer function described in Chapter 8 is carried out. Exit *A* for this function indicates

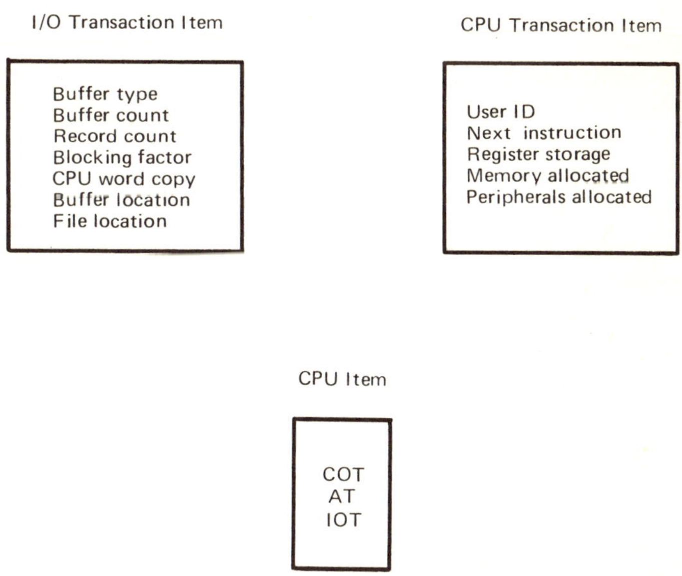

Fig. 33. I/O and CPU Transactions

that the next record location sought by the I/O transaction is available, and that there is at least one more record location available in the current buffer block. Exit *B* indicates that the next record location is available; it is, however, the last record location in the current buffer block. Exit *C* indicates that no record location is available in the referenced buffer for the I/O transaction. The parameter "one" is chosen if the function is to handle a type one buffer, and the parameter "two" is chosen if the buffer function is to handle a type two buffer.

Copy (Queue/Place Name) Into (Queue/Place Name)

The contents of a specified queue location or a specified memory location are copied into the specified queue or memory location. The queue locations involved are the current positions of queue pointers. If the "place name" parameter is chosen, then the memory location referred to may be the AT, IOT, or any other symbolic location. Unless the AT or IOT locations of the CPU item are named as parameters of this operator, there is no effect on the CPU term due to its execution. If either parameter of this operator refers to attributes in the CPU or transaction items, then the operator must be entered with CPU and I/O words in the AT or IOT positions of the CPU term in order to designate the particular item of either type under reference.

Cycle

In an actual machine, this operator would be a one instruction transfer loop, and represents a point of waiting on the part of the CPU. The operator also enables the I/O termination interrupts, so that once a COT enters this operator it may only exit via an interrupt. In general, the contents of the CPU item are arbitrary on entering this operator. However, as will be seen below in the example, exit from the operator via an I/O termination interrupt may destroy the current contents of the AT location.

Delete (Queue/Place Name)

The indicated location is set to zero on execution of this operator. If the parameter reference is to a CPU or I/O transaction item, then the CPU term on entering this operator must indicate the presence of an AT or IOT as required.

Increment Buffer Count

This operator is entered with an I/O word in the IOT location of the CPU item. The buffer count associated with the I/O transaction represented by this I/O word is incremented by unity on execution of this operator.

Match (AT/IOT) Against (Queue/Place Name)

If a queue name is specified for the second parameter, then each item in the queue, starting with the logical first item and in the logical order of the queue (LIFO, FIFO, or priority) is matched for equality against the contents of the AT or IOT location of the CPU item. There are two exits associated with this operator. If no match is found, then one of these exits is taken. If a match is found, then the second exit is taken, and in the case of a queue it is assumed that a pointer for this queue is set to indicate the matching item. In the case of a place name used as the second parameter of this operator, the match is made against a named memory location. If this parameter refers to a location in the CPU or I/O transaction item, then the operator will refer to the contents of the AT or IOT positions of the CPU term, as required.

O/S

This operator has been defined earlier. Its function is to move the COT into the AT location (any present CPU word in that location will be destroyed) and to retrieve the operating system transaction, *Z*, storing it in the COT location. The contents of the IOT location are not affected. In addition, further I/O interrupts are disabled. It is assumed that the hardware will retain interrupts occurring while the interrupt mechanism is disabled. so that these may be presented to the system when enabled at a later time.

Place (AT/IOT) Into (Queue/Place Name)

This operator is entered with either a CPU or I/O word in the AT or IOT location as specified by the first parameter. Its function is to move the designated contents of the CPU item into the specified queue or place name. The specified location of the CPU item is replaced with zero. If the second parameter is a place name in the CPU or I/O transaction item, then the CPU term on entrance to this operator must have respectively an AT or IOT as the available transaction. The AT or IOT location, as specified, is replaced by zero.

Place IOT Into (Queue Name) by Channel

This operator is entered with an I/O word in the IOT location of the CPU item. This word is then moved into the designated queue, where it is assumed that the queue name is generic for all queues associated with I/O channels. Thus, channel 1 might be associated with IQ1 (Initation Queue 1), channel 2 with IQ2, and so on. The IOT location of the CPU item is replaced by zero.

Return (COT/AT)

The return operator has been discussed earlier. If the COT parameter is selected, then return is made to the worker program last executed by the current operating transaction. If the AT parameter is selected, the return is made to the worker program last executed by the available transaction. In the first instance, there is no effect on the AT and IOT locations of the CPU item. In the second instance, however, the contents of the COT location are replaced by the contents of the AT location, and the AT location is set to zero. The IOT location of the CPU item is not effected. In addition, I/O termination interrupts are enabled.

Select (AT/IOT) From (Queue/Place Name)

If a queue name is selected for the second parameter, this operator selects the logical first item in the queue and places it into either the AT or IOT location of the CPU item as designated by the first parameter. If a place name is designated as the point of selection, then the transfer is made directly. In either event, the current contents of the AT or IOT, as designated in the first parameter of the operator, are replaced by the selected transaction word and therefore are lost. The position of the selected transaction in either queue or place name is set to zero. If the contents of a place name is zero, or if the queue is empty, then a separate exit is made from this operator.

Select IOT From (Queue Name) by Channel

It is assumed that a designation of the channel of interest is determined by interrupt and supplied by the hardware on execution of this operator. One of the several queues associated with the set of channels is thus the source of I/O transaction words, with selection made according to the criteria established for the queue. The current contents of the IOT location of the CPU item are then replaced by the selected I/O word, and its position in the queue set to zero.

Start I/O

This operator is entered with an I/O word in the IOT location of the CPU item. The actual transfer of data between the specified buffer and associated peripheral device is then initiated by this operator.

Step (Queue Name)

The pointer associated with the indicated queue is stepped to the logical next position by this operator.

Test Buffer Type

This operator is entered with an I/O word in the IOT location of the CPU item. By referring to the indicated I/O transaction item, the buffer type for the file associated with this I/O word is determined. There are two exits from this operator. The first is taken if the buffer is determined to be of type one, and the second if it is of type two.

Test IOT (Channel/Device)

This operator is entered with an I/O word in the IOT location of the CPU item. The channel, or device, as indicated by the parameter that is associated with the buffer assigned to the I/O word, is then tested for its availability. There are two exits from this operator, the first being taken if the channel or device, as specified, is not busy, the second if busy.

The Prototype MPX

The logic of a multiprogram executive capable of handling buffered execution of worker programs in the multiprogram set is given in the transaction charts of Figs. 34 and 35. There are two entrances of interest to MPX. The first of these is the I/O request entrance and the second is the I/O termination interrupt entrance.

I/O Request

When a worker transaction executes an I/O request, it is brought to the operating system where its buffer type is determined, and then the buffer state ascertained for the particular buffer associated with the referenced I/O operation. If the next record location is available to the worker program, then an immediate return is made. If the next record location is available to the worker program but exhausts record locations in the current buffer block, then an attempt to initiate the requested input or output activity for that buffer is made, and, if successful, return to the calling worker transaction occurs directly. If the I/O operation cannot be instituted at this time, the I/O transaction word is placed into the proper initiation queue and return to the calling worker transaction is made. In the event that there are no records available in the buffer being referenced, it is assumed that a prior I/O activity has been initiated relative to this buffer, and the worker transaction's further execution is deferred. This deferred transaction remains in this state until the input or output activity relative to the buffer to which reference has just been made is completed. When this occurs, the worker transaction will be removed from deferred status and be made available again for execution. When the further execution of a worker transaction is deferred under these circumstances, it is then necessary for MPX to select some other worker transaction from the availability queue as the current operating transaction.

The logic required for operating the I/O request entrance to MPX is shown in transaction chart 34. The entrance is made at box 1 where the COT is *W*; the worker transaction makes the I/O request. Its execution of the I/O statement in its program

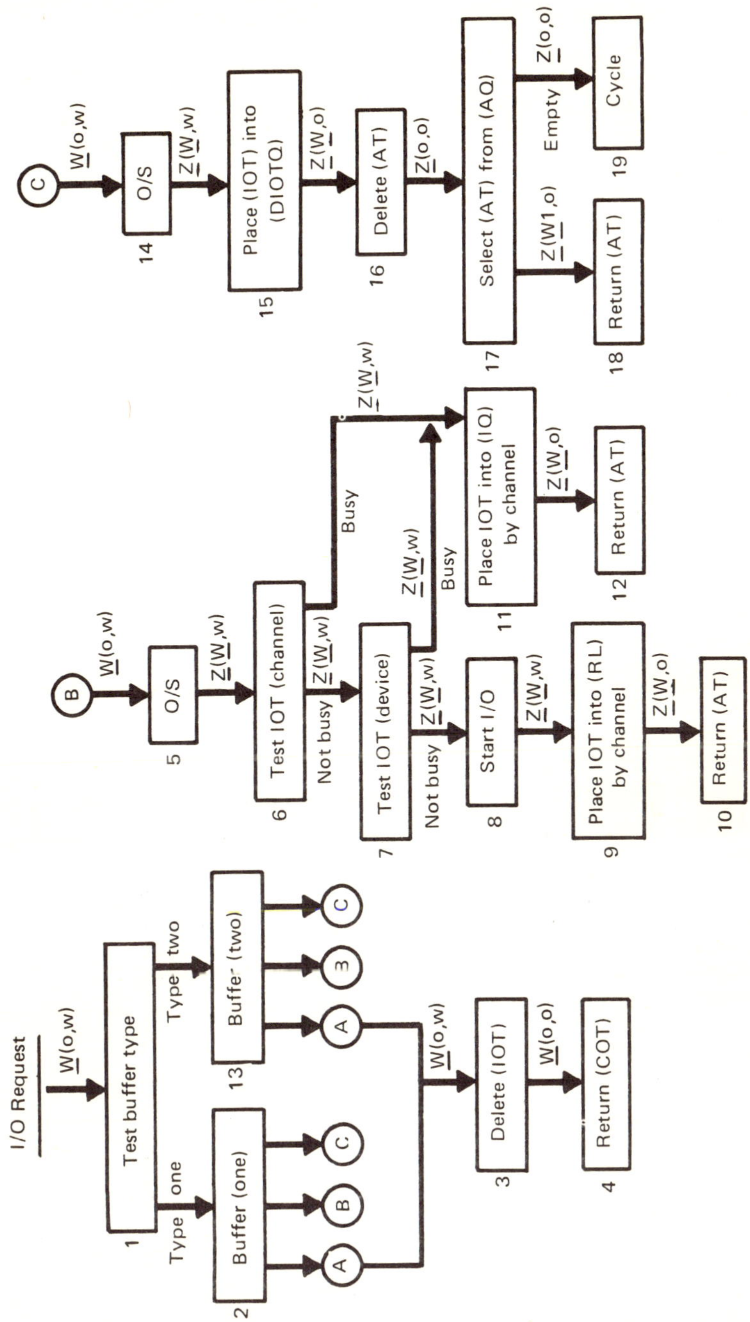

Fig. 34. I/O Request Entrance

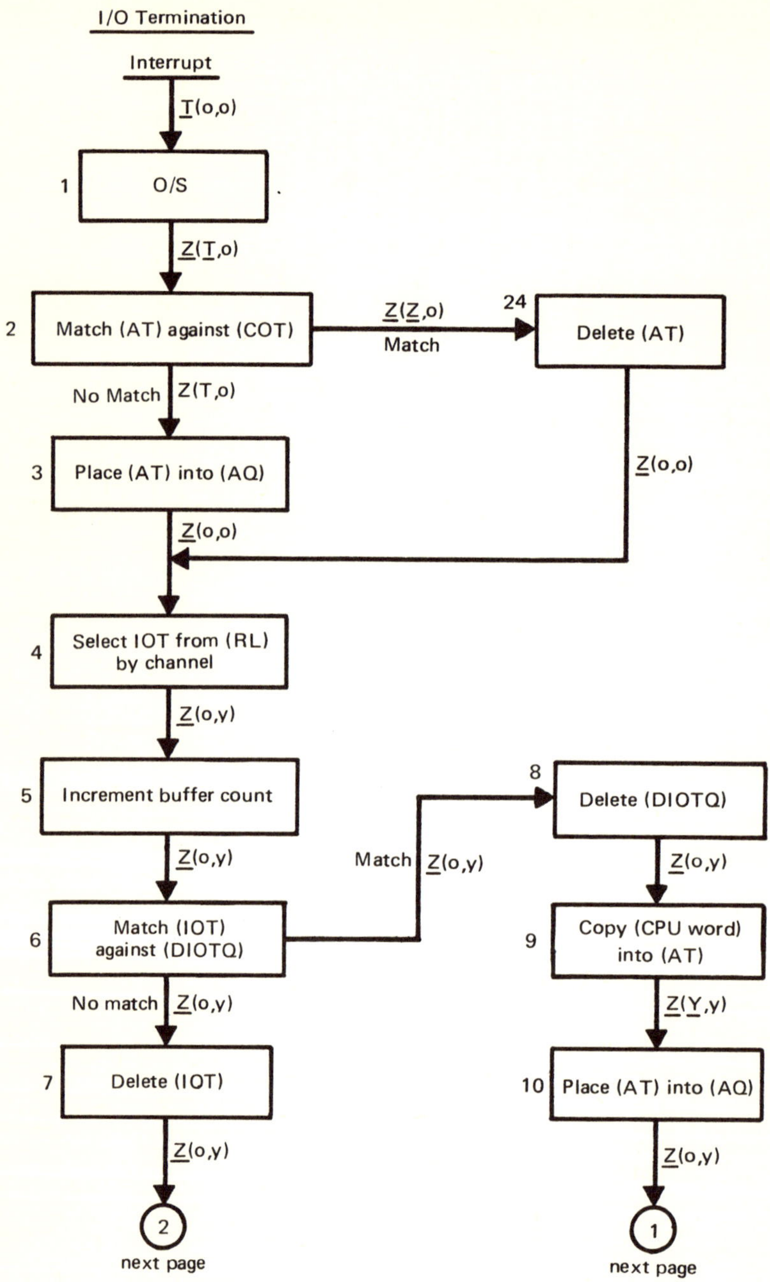

Fig. 35. I/O Termination Interrupt Entrance

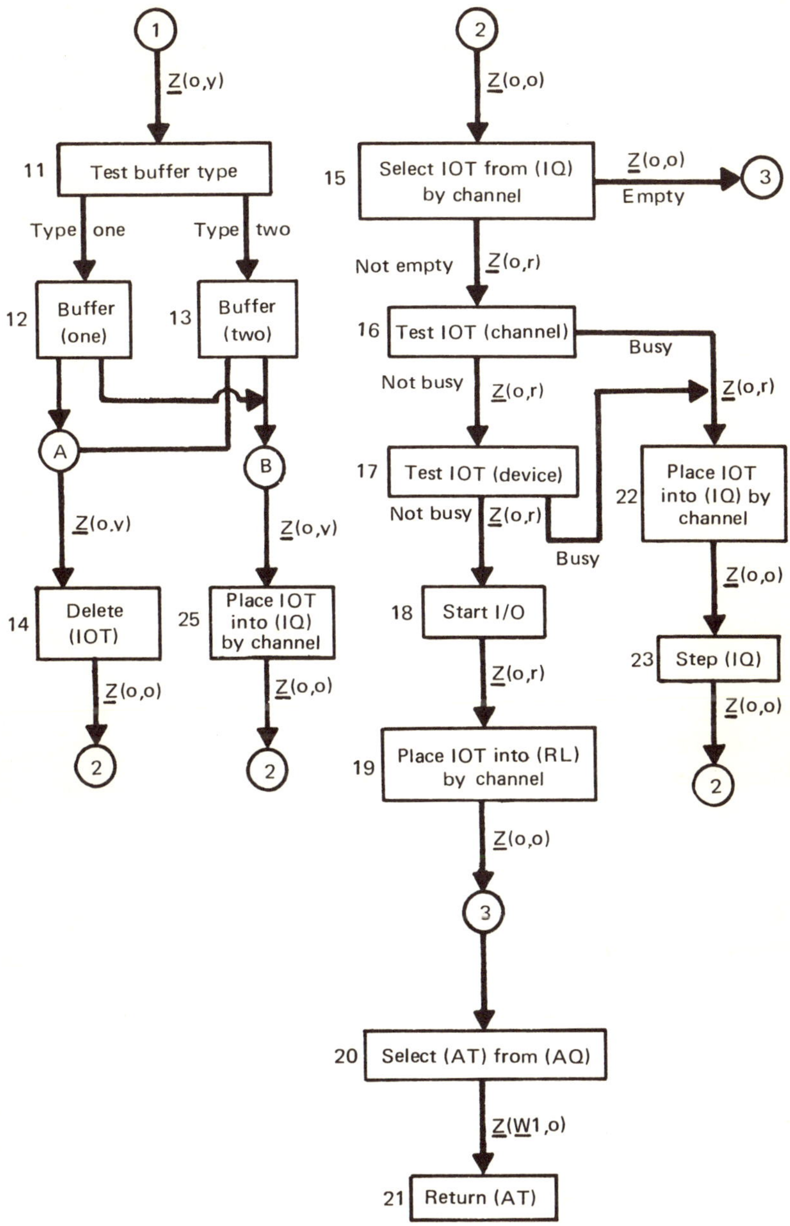

Fig. 35. Continued

has created the I/O word, *w*, as indicated in the CPU term on entrance to box 1.

The first operation determines the type of buffer being referred to by the IOT and transfers to either box 2 or box 13 depending on the results of this test, as indicated in the transaction chart. There is no change in the CPU term.

The buffer operators of boxes 2 and 13 ascertain the state of the buffer referred to by the IOT. If this buffer is in the *A* state, then transfer is made to box 3.

On entrance to box 3, it has been ascertained by the buffer function that the next record location in the current buffer block is available (in the case of a type one buffer, the record has been delivered or emplaced), and that there exists at least one more record location available in this block. Hence, the CPU transaction, *W*, may continue with its execution. However, at this point, the IOT, having served its function, is extraneous, and therefore the purpose of box 3 is to delete *w* by setting the IOT location of the CPU item to zero. This is indicated on exit from box 3.

Since *W* is the current operating transaction (the operating system entrance boundary has not been crossed) the operator in box 4 returns to the COT, thereby resuming the execution by the CPU transaction *W*.

In the case where the execution of the buffer operator of box 2 or 13 designates that the buffer referred to by the IOT is in the *B* state, transfer is made for entrance to box 5. This is the operating system entrance boundary, and the transformation it effects on the CPU item is shown in the CPU term on exit from box 5. Here *Z* has replaced *W* as the COT, *W* has become the available transaction, and *w* remains as the IOT. Also, further termination interrupts are disabled.

The next operator at box 6 tests the channel associated with the buffer referred to by the IOT, *w*. If this channel is not busy, i.e. available, then in box 7 a test for the availability of the device holding the file associated with the buffer referred to by the IOT is made. If the device is available as well, then at box 8 the required input/output operation is started.

Note that the above operations in no way alter the CPU

term. Hence, on entrance to box 9, having initiated the input/output required at this point by the IOT, the I/O word it contains is placed into the reference list according to the channel it is now using. It is from this position that this I/O word will be retrieved when a termination signal for this channel next occurs.

Part of the function of the operator in box 9, once the IOT has been moved from the CPU item, is to set the IOT location to zero. This is indicated in the CPU term on exit from box 9.

At this point, the next record location has been made available to the calling CPU transaction *W*. This record has emptied (or filled) a buffer block associated with *W*, and, as described above, a data transfer between this block and its peripheral device has been initiated. Therefore, at this point return can be made to the available CPU transaction, *W*, to continue its execution. This operator also enables the I/O termination interrupts.

Returning now to boxes 6 and 7, and assuming that either the required channel or device for the IOT, *w*, were not available, a transfer to box 11 will occur. In this case, it is not possible to initiate the actual data transfer at this time, and therefore, at box 11, the IOT is placed into the initiation queue by channel, from which position it will be selected when the channel it seeks next becomes available. This operation sets the IOT location of the CPU item to zero as indicated in the CPU term on exit from box 11.

At this point, the I/O requested by the CPU transaction *W* has been honored in that a record has been delivered (or emplaced), and, in addition, the I/O transaction, *w*, has been placed into the proper initiation queue. It then remains in that queue until a termination interrupt on the channel it seeks occurs, at which time a new attempt to initiate the actual data transfer will be undertaken. With these operations accomplished the CPU transaction *W* may continue its execution. This is accomplished at box 12 by returning to the available transaction.

Returning to box 2 (or box 13), consider the case where the next record location in the buffer designated by the IOT is not available. In this case, the buffer is determined to be in the *C* state, and therefore transfer is made to box 14.

Box 14 represents an entrance boundary to the operating system, and therefore the CPU transaction, *W*, is replaced as the COT by the operating system transaction, *Z*. The I/O termination interrupts are disabled, *W* becomes the available transaction, and there is no change in the IOT.

At this point in the logic of MPX, it is necessary to defer any further use of the I/O transaction, *w*, and any further execution by the worker transaction, *W*. Since there is no record position available in the buffer associated with the IOT, it must be assumed that a prior I/O request found that buffer in the *B* state, and through the course of action described above, created the necessary data transfer which at this time has yet to be completed, i.e. the transfer may be underway, or the associated I/O word may still be in the initiation queue. Therefore, at box 15 the IOT representing the current requirement on this buffer is placed into a queue of deferred IOT's, DIOTQ, there to await that I/O termination which signals that a data transfer between its buffer and peripheral device has been completed. When that occurs, the deferred I/O transaction word will be retrieved from DIOTQ and used to complete the current I/O request for the CPU transaction *W*.

The I/O transaction currently being used to represent data transfer between the associated buffer and its peripheral device will later be used, when that data transfer has been completed, to retrieve the CPU word copy from the I/O transaction item so that it may be made available for further execution. This is the reason for retaining a copy of the parent CPU transaction word in the I/O transaction item, as indicated in Fig. 33. Hence, at this point in the logic of MPX, it is sufficient to simply get rid of the available transaction, *W*, since a copy of it is available in the I/O transaction item for *w* as the "CPU word copy." Therefore, the operator of box 16 deletes the AT, leaving the CPU term as shown.

At this point, both the IOT and the parent worker transaction which generated it have been deferred from further execution.

It is now the task of MPX to select a next COT from among those seeking access to the CPU. These transactions are located in the availability queue (AQ). This is the function of the operator in box 17, and if there exists at least one transaction word in the AQ, then on exit from box 17 the selected transaction appears as the AT in the CPU item, as shown in the transaction chart. With this accomplished, execution by the selected CPU transaction is continued via the return operator in box 18.

In the event that the availability queue is empty at this time, a transfer is made from box 17 to box 19. Note that there has been no change in the CPU term due to the fact that there were no available CPU transactions in the AQ. Hence, the CYCLE operator of box 19 is entered. It enables the I/O termination interrupts and cycles the CPU. The CPU then remains in a waiting state until an I/O termination interrupt releases a deferred worker transaction and places it into the availability queue. When this occurs, the operating system transaction, *Z*, can continue its execution of MPX, ultimately reaching a point where a selection is made from the availability queue.

I/O Termination Interrupt

The I/O termination interrupt is the second entrance of major importance to MPX. When such an interrupt occurs, the interrupted worker transaction is placed back into the availability queue so that it remains available for selection as the next current operating transaction. Then the I/O transaction word for the data transfer, whose completion is signaled by this termination interrupt, is retrieved from the associated channel word in the reference list. This I/O transaction is used to increase the buffer count in its I/O transaction item, and then to determine if its parent CPU transaction has been previously deferred from further execution until this data transfer has been completed. If this is discovered to be the case, the CPU word for the deferred transaction is placed into the availability queue, thus making it available for selection as the next COT. Furthermore, the deferred I/O transaction is honored so that the record sought by the CPU transaction, and whose unavailability caused it earlier to be deferred, is now made available to that transaction. On the other hand, if the I/O transaction whose data transfer has just terminated was not responsible for its parent CPU transaction's being deferred, then the next steps are to investigate the initiation queue for the channel of which the data transfer has just completed for any I/O transactions awaiting access to this channel. Once these steps have been accomplished, the final operation of MPX for this entrance is to select a next current operating transaction from the availability queue.

The details of these operations are shown in Fig. 35, and begin with the interrupted CPU transaction, *T*, crossing the operating system entrance boundary at box 1. This makes the operating system transaction, *Z*, the current operating transaction, and makes *T* the available transaction. In addition, further I/O interrupts are disabled.

From the earlier description of the I/O request entrance to MPX, it will be recalled that, failing to find an entry on the availability queue, the transaction, *Z*, goes into a cycle operation with the I/O termination interrupts enabled. In such a case, when the I/O termination interrupt occurs, *Z* will be the interrupted transaction. It is the purpose of the operator at box 2 to ascertain whether or not this is indeed the situation. This is accomplished by matching the AT against the COT. If the system was cycling at the time of the I/O termination interrupt, then the CPU transaction, *T*, appearing in the CPU term on entrance to box 2 will actually be the operating system transaction, *Z*, and will exactly match the COT. This causes the indicated transfer to box 24 where the AT is simply deleted.

On the other hand, if the operating system were not cycling at the time of the interrupt, then the interrupted transaction is associated with a worker program, and therefore no match will occur. In this case, the operator in box 3 places the available transaction, i.e. the worker transaction interrupted by the I/O termination, into the availability queue so that it remains eligible for selection as the next COT.

In either case described, then, the CPU term on entrance to box 4 shows that no AT or IOT is present. Therefore, the next step is to retrieve the I/O transaction word associated with the

I/O termination interrupt. This is to be found in the reference list (RL) word for the terminating channel, and the operator at box 4 carries this out. This results in an available IOT, as shown in the CPU term on exit from box 4.

With the I/O transaction for the terminated data transfer available, the operator at box 5 causes the associated I/O transaction item to have its buffer count incremented by unity, thereby indicating that an additional block is available to the CPU transaction that generated this I/O transaction. Box 5 has no effect on the CPU term.

The next step is to determine if some worker transaction had been previously deferred from further execution while awaiting completion of the data transfer represented by the IOT. It will be recalled that when a worker transaction seeks access to a record location in a buffer that it is in the *C* state, its further execution is deferred, and, in addition, the I/O word that it has generated is placed into the deferred IOT queue, DIOTQ. Therefore, if the I/O word representing the terminating data transfer is associated with this same buffer, the match of IOT against DIOTQ will be successful. In this case, the transaction chart shows a transfer to box 8. Note that the operator of box 6 does not effect the CPU term.

Assume that the IOT finds a match in DIOTQ. Then the operator of a box 8 deletes the deferred I/O transaction in DIOTQ since the present IOT, which is identical to it and which has served its purpose relative to its own I/O request, can now be used to represent this deferred I/O request. At box 9, the CPU word copy of the I/O transaction item, which is identical to the parent CPU transaction word (earlier deleted as part of the deferment process, box 16, Fig. 34) is then copied into the AT location of the CPU item. This demonstrates the requirement for the presence of the CPU word in each I/O transaction item, since at the point in the logic of MPX where the CPU word is required the only information relating to the specific parent transaction is the IOT. This designates its I/O transaction item in which is found a copy of its parent CPU word. Thus, on exit from box 9, the CPU term indicates that the parent CPU transaction, here shown as *Y*, is now the AT.

Since the parent CPU transaction is now released from its deferred status, it is placed in the availability queue, thereby making it eligible for selection as the next COT. This is accomplished by the operator in box 10, and leaves the CPU term as shown on exit from that box.

At this point, the IOT represents the still to be honored I/O request that earlier caused the parent CPU transaction to be deferred from further execution. Therefore, it is necessary to treat this I/O request so that the record originally sought by the parent transaction is now made available to it (delivered or emplaced, depending on whether the buffer is for input or output, respectively). To accomplish this requires the execution of the buffer operator, and the operator at box 11 determines the buffer type associated with the IOT, and executes either box 12 or box 13 according to this determination.

Since the entrance to MPX at this time has been for an I/O termination representing a data transfer that is completed relative to the buffer associated with the IOT, that buffer cannot be in the *C* state. On the other hand, if the blocking factor is greater than one, i.e. there are two or more records per block, then clearly the buffer must be in the *A* state. In this case, box 14 is the next operator executed.

However, if the blocking factor is one so that there is only a single record per block, then the buffer will be in the *B* state, and therefore box 25 is next executed. In the former case, since the IOT has served its purpose, it is sufficient to delete it, leaving the CPU term without an AT or IOT, after which transfer to box 15 is accomplished. However, if the blocking factor is one record per block, then the execution of box 25 places the IOT into the initiation queue by channel. Again this leaves the CPU term with no AT or IOT as shown, and transfer in this case is made to box 15 as well.

We pause here to recapitulate the consequences of the execution of MPX to this point. In the first place, if the interrupted CPU transaction was associated with a worker program, it has been placed into the availability queue so that it remains eligible for selection as the next COT. The I/O word representing the terminated data transfer is retrieved and used to increment the buffer count of its associated I/O transaction item. It is then employed to determine if its parent CPU transaction had been earlier deferred from further execution by virtue of its having found this buffer in the *C* state on the occasion of its last I/O request. This is accomplished by matching the IOT against the deferred IOT queue. If there is no match, than either the parent CPU transaction is not deferred at all (in which case it appears in the AQ), or the parent transaction is indeed deferred, but this deferment was due to having found someone of its other buffers in the *C* state. In this second instance, it must await the termination of the I/O associated with that particular buffer for its release from the deferred status. In either event, the failure of the match of IOT against DIOTQ implies that no action need be taken at this time for the release of the parent CPU transaction. Hence, the IOT, having accomplished all its functions, is deleted. If, however, the parent CPU transaction has indeed been deferred pending the completion of this current data transfer, the CPU word is copied from the I/O transaction item and placed into the availability queue, thereby making it eligible for selection as the next COT. The next step then is to use the IOT to represent the deferred I/O request, and to honor that I/O request, initiating the next input/output activity if that is required by the current state of this buffer. In all events, each of these contingencies leads to connector 2 of the transaction chart of Fig. 35, with the CPU term as shown.

At box 15, the logical first entry in the initiation queue associated with the terminating channel is selected, given that there is an entry in that queue (if box 25 was the last operator executed, then indeed there is as least one entry in that queue). Then a transfer is made to box 16 and thence to boxes 17, 18, 19, or to box 22 where, as described earlier, an attempt to initiate the I/O associated with the selected IOT is made. If successful, then the input/output activity is started by the operator in box 18, and the IOT is placed into the reference list by channel, as shown in box 19. If, however, it is not possible to start the I/O for this selected IOT at this time, it is returned to its initiation queue, and the logical next location in that queue is then set as the point of selection by the operator of box 23, after which there is a return to box 15.

This cycle from box 15 through box 23 is repeated until either an IOT has been selected from the initiation queue associated with the terminating channel which can have its I/O operation initiated, or all members of that queue have been examined, in which case the "empty" exit from box 16 is taken. This causes a transfer to connector 3 and a subsequent entrance to box 20.

At this point, all operations relative to initiating a new input/output activity on the terminating channel have been accomplished, and the next and final steps by MPX are, at box 20, to select the next COT from the availability queue, making it the available transaction, and then to return, at box 21, to this available transaction, thereby resuming its execution. This operator also enables the I/O termination interrupts.

INDEX